Praise for
Turning Your Down into Up

"*Turning Your Down into Up* is a comprehensive, whole-person approach to curing depression. Dr. Jantz offers an encouraging and practical recovery plan, with new answers and hope for the healing journey through depression."

—Dr. Catherine Hart Weber, author of *Flourish: Discover the Daily Joy of Abundant, Vibrant Living*

"I found this book full of hope for souls struggling to find light in the midst of the darkness of a clinical depression. I also found it refreshing from the perspective that it presents a new and bold approach to the ancient problem of depression. The book presents what the authors refer to as a Whole Person Treatment plan that has been practiced and proven effective within Dr. Jantz's personal treatment organization, The Center near Seattle, WA. The whole person refers to the patient's emotional, environmental, physical, and spiritual self. The treatment plan involves the exploration of each of these four areas of the depressed person's life and then helps them own their feelings, understand how their past or present environment has contributed to their depression, discover what role their physical health can hold in their depression and recovery, and finally, assess where they are or need to be spiritually, to move out of their darkness into light or turn their down into up. I agree with the concept and the directions for recovery this book has to offer. It offers the hope the authors intend it to."

—Dr. Freda V. Crews, DMin, PhD, and television host of *Time for Hope*

"There's no shortage of books on depression. What makes this one stand out is its 'whole-person' approach. Based on decades of experience, Dr. Greg Jantz shows readers how to create a week-by-week, personalized recovery plan…and explore valuable options beyond 'medicate it' or 'get over it.' If you're seeking practical, workable solutions to overcoming depression, read on!"

—June Hunt, founder, CEO, CSO (Chief Servant Officer)
Hope for the Heart, and author of *How to Handle Your Emotions*

Turning Your Down into Up

Turning Your Down into Up

A Realistic Plan for Healing from Depression

Gregory L. Jantz, PhD,
with Ann McMurray

Revised and Updated: Previously released as *Moving Beyond Depression*

WATERBROOK
PRESS

Turning Your Down into Up
Published by WaterBrook Press
12265 Oracle Boulevard, Suite 200
Colorado Springs, Colorado 80921

Trade Paperback ISBN: 978-0-307-73210-1
eBook ISBN: 978-0-307-73211-8

Originally published under the title *Moving Beyond Depression.*

Published in the United States by WaterBrook Multnomah, an imprint of the Crown Publishing Group, a division of Random House Inc., New York.

WATERBROOK and its deer colophon are registered trademarks of Random House Inc.

Library of Congress Cataloging-in-Publication Data
Jantz, Gregory L.
    Turning your down into up : a realistic plan for healing from depression / by Gregory L. Jantz, PhD, with Ann McMurray.—First Edition.
        pages cm
    Includes bibliographical references.
    ISBN 978-0-307-73210-1—ISBN 978-0-307-73211-8 (electronic) 1. Depression, Mental—Popular works. 2. Depression, Mental—Alternative treatment—Popular works. I. Title.
    RC537. J358 2013
    616.85'27—dc23
                                                        2013003149

Printed in the United States of America
2013—First Edition

10 9 8 7 6 5 4 3 2 1

SPECIAL SALES
Most WaterBrook Multnomah books are available at special quantity discounts when purchased in bulk by corporations, organizations, and special-interest groups. Custom imprinting or excerpting can also be done to fit special needs. For information, please e-mail SpecialMarkets@WaterBrookMultnomah.com or call 1-800-603-7051.

To all whom the cloud of depression has
not yet lifted, there is hope.
Let's walk together through these pages on
a journey that brings great rewards.
May you sense a new direction and peace.

 Contents

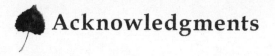 # Acknowledgments

To the steadfast team at the Center who have mapped out the vision of hope for nearly thirty years. And to my WaterBrook family and editor Bruce Nygren, I am grateful for his gift of "perfection."

Not Just a Case of the Blues

Depression is on the rise, according to the World Health Organization. The phenomenon isn't contained within the borders of the United States or confined to the technological frontiers of the First World. Across the globe, by the year 2020, depression will be second only to heart disease as the leading cause of debilitating illness. It's everywhere; it's increasing; it's serious. This isn't just a global case of the blues.

If you ask people on the street if they know someone who has suffered from heart problems, they will probably tell about an uncle or a parent who has had a heart attack, angioplasty, or bypass surgery. In some cases, that person may no longer be alive. But often, the patient will have recovered and is reportedly "doing great."

Ask them if they know someone who has suffered from depression, and they may not answer as quickly. Most will probably be able to come up with someone. They may remember an aunt who always seemed unhappy at family functions, if she showed up at all. They may recall a cousin who was depressed in high school. They will probably be hesitant to conclude the person is doing well. Instead, they tend to adopt a more watchful, wait-and-see attitude. In fact, according to the World Health Organization, depression is a leading disability worldwide, affecting more than 350 million people.[1]

At the facility I founded, the Center for Counseling and Health Resources near Seattle, Washington, people come to us with fears, doubts, nonexistent motivation, and a general lack of vitality in their lives. The hope and optimism of childhood seem a distant, ill-remembered dream as they venture through adulthood. At the Center, we recognize these symptoms of depression and work to stem its tide in those we counsel. Society doesn't always make our job easier.

People often mention the late Kurt Cobain (1967–94) when discussing depression. Kurt, the lead singer for the grunge group Nirvana, was said to be the voice of his generation, a harbinger of their feelings, thoughts, and emotions. In his life, Cobain articulated the tragic results of failing to recover from his long-standing depression. Never choosing to whitewash his despair, Cobain instead embraced his dark feelings and responded to an uncomprehending world with his signature album *Nevermind*. His obsessive self-hatred and destructive attempts at self-medication through drugs, alcohol, and inner rage resulted in his successful suicide in 1994. Clearly, in his life and even in his death, Cobain was on the leading edge of societal trends.

More recently, we have publicly witnessed the fatal consequences of depression surrounding the high-profile deaths of musicians Michael Jackson and Amy Winehouse, model Anna Nicole Smith, and actors Heath Ledger and Brittany Murphy. Though other factors certainly played into their troubling lives and tragic deaths, the medication of depression only compounded the problem, in some cases *self*-medicating behaviors; in others, prescribed antidepressants may have been either ineffective or simply done more harm than good in combination with other drugs.

Though the media focus on their lives often spills over into the absurd, celebrity struggles with depression shine a sobering spotlight on how difficult depression is to treat, even for those who have every resource imaginable at their disposal.

Out with the Old

Depression is becoming more pervasive, and with its increase, professionals are scrambling to craft a response. While there is a growing recognition that the old answers aren't working anymore, health-care experts agree the answer is not in continuing the wholesale medication of both children and adults. But neither should sufferers be left to concoct their own destructive, self-medicating strategies.

In the past, there were two popular responses to depression: get over it or medicate it. Those suffering with depression were considered to be self-indulgent and self-obsessed. Their dark moods were responded to with little patience or understanding. People with depression were often counseled to just "Cheer up!" When the "get-over-it" method didn't seem to work, increasing numbers of sufferers turned to medication. The use of Prozac and other antidepressant medications has recently skyrocketed.

For those choosing to medicate their way out of depression, some have used prescription medication, and others have medicated their pain with age-old remedies such as alcoholism, drug abuse, promiscuity, eating disorders, self-mutilation, and other compulsive behaviors. In recent years, a new addiction has reared its ugly head: addiction to new media and technology, a welcome distraction from reality that is not only socially acceptable but encouraged and celebrated. Some retreat to addictions, and some retreat to lethargy and sleep, unable to get out of bed in the morning, day after day.

Frustration over the inability to deal with depression has increased also, not only among health-care professionals but also among those who suffer from it. When depressed people are unable to pull themselves up by their mental bootstraps, so to speak, and prescribed medication and even self-medication aren't successful, many conclude that suicide is the only way out of their downward spiral. Victims of ongoing depression often feel that life no longer seems worth living. Their struggle to survive simple daily tasks just doesn't seem worth the pain.

One Story, Different Voices

As depression increases, it rises to the top of our national consciousness, out from the shadows and into the spotlight. As more people become aware of depression, they recognize its presence in their own lives. The nameless dread, the constant fear, the ever-present weight takes on a name. It has now become a "diagnosis."

With the identification of a diagnosis comes the desire for a one-size-fits-all solution. A singular reason, with a scientific solution, is appealing to the depressed individual and to his or her concerned family, friends, or acquaintances. When the reason for depression is understood—especially in light of new discoveries in brain science—there is a new sense of hope for its treatment. If we know what the problem is, we believe our technological society should be able to fix it. Energized by the discovery of a reason for destructive behaviors, many sufferers become impatient for a "cure," hence the current increase in pharmaceutical remedies for the symptoms of depression.

When individuals acknowledge their depression and say, "Yes, that's my problem," they can feel as if identifying their problem also solves it. But understanding the problem of depression doesn't mean the journey to healing is over. The diagnosis of depression in a person's life is more like a crossroad than a single destination.

People arrive at the point of depression from many different places, indicating there are a variety of paths to recovery. In short, there is no *one* answer for depression and no *single* path to recovery. Just as the reasons for depression are as varied as the individuals who suffer from it, the paths to recovery will also be unique to each individual.

Not every person suffering from depression should be medicated.

Not every person who has a bad day is depressed.

Not every person who struggles over meaning and purpose in life should be viewed as "crazy."

Not every person is able to bounce back from a major traumatic event without assistance.

In order to deal with an individual's depression, his or her uniqueness, his or her story must be heard, understood, and integrated into a personalized recovery.

The Whole-Person Approach

Applying the whole-person approach to recovery can individualize treatment for depression. The whole-person approach is based upon recognition of the unique components of an individual's life and how these components interweave to form the whole person. This book is designed to explain each component of the whole-person approach and how those components can identify real answers to curing depression.

The components we will look at in the whole-person approach are emotional, environmental, relational, physical, and spiritual. Together, these components provide keys to why a person is depressed, and they can open a doorway to his or her recovery.

Emotional Influences

We are emotional beings, and we choose to acknowledge or express those emotions in outward forms. We are never far from our feelings and emotions. They trip us up when we are stressed or tired. They sneak up on us at unexpected moments. They support our expectations, fuel our disappointments, and energize our victories.

When depression settles into a person's life, emotions become confused. A promotion at work may produce thoughts of despair and fear. Minor daily irritants can become major life hurdles. The joy of others can become a gloomy reminder of inner insecurities. Even if life appears to be going well, our emotional balance can become tilted toward depression, at the mercy of the dangerous balancing act of anger, fear, shame, and guilt.

Environmental Influences

We live in a world where complexity greets us every morning. What are we going to wear? What are we going to eat? How are we going to get to work? Which tasks are we going to complete? What calls are we going to

deal with first? Should we answer our cell phone, our home phone, respond to our e-mail, reply to our voice mail, check and update our social
networks—and in what order? From the moment we awake, the assault
begins. We are overwhelmed. The assault demands a response, and retreating into depression can be that response.

Relational Influences

We constantly use relationships to determine our position in life. We
observe the world and people around us and make decisions about who
we are based on how we believe others perceive us. We define our position
by the people with whom we interact—online and off, which can be, and
often are, two different dynamics altogether as we tend to mask our real
selves behind our virtual personas. We use this information to triangulate
our state of well-being, factoring in what we've learned or observed in the
past, a view of our present circumstances, and the potential outcome for
our future.

Depending on our ability to reason truthfully, these relationships
provide us with a sense of well-being or foreboding. The uniqueness of
our circumstances and our relationships can either help or hinder our
ability to deal with these ever-present thoughts and emotions.

Physical Influences

In the past, the answer to a broken-down spirit was a pharmaceutical
"fix" that relaxed the physical body. But as we learn more and more about
brain science and depression, as well as the interworking of mind, body,
and spirit, we are learning that the potential exists for our bodies to act as
partners in recovery instead of as opponents.

Spiritual Influences

Wrestling with questions of worth and purpose are spiritual issues. *Who
am I? What is my purpose? Where is joy? When will this be over? Why is this
happening? How did I get this way?* The spiritual component of a person's

life can provide direction toward both the right questions and the needed answers.

Finding Your Story, Finding Your Way

If you suffer from light to severe depression, this book is designed to help you articulate your feelings, define your questions, and uncover your unique answers that will lead you to recovery from its oppression. There is no one-size-fits-all answer for depression, but there is one that's just right for you.

You may choose to study this book with a caring professional, someone who can assist you in your recovery process, or you may be determined enough to read through this book on your own. Whenever possible and appropriate, please consider working through this material with another person who is equipped to assist you in understanding your depression and is willing to walk this journey of recovery with you.

Take time to read over each section. It may be that one section seems targeted to your individual situation, but every component of this whole-person approach will impact your recovery. Allow yourself the time to read each section carefully and examine how their integrated truths apply to your whole person.

To assist you in processing the information presented in this book and your reaction to it, I suggest that you use a journal throughout your reading. There will be opportunities for you to specifically use the journal, and there will be times when a thought or concept impacts your own situation with special emphasis. While these insights resonate, write them down. Put in writing the truth, as you understand it. Write down how you are feeling as you work through this truth. Write down what motivates you to act. In this way, you'll be writing your own book of recovery.

This book is for you and about you.

Now before we investigate the new answers to depression, read through the following section to evaluate whether or not depression is influencing the quality of your life.

Depression Indicators

When her supervisor asked to see her, Karen felt a nervous twinge in her stomach. Walking to her boss's office, she reviewed the last several months and wondered if she had done something wrong. Employees usually didn't get called into the supervisor's office unless some costly mistake had happened. She silently hoped that a coworker hadn't made a complaint against her. Karen's anxiety intensified as she neared the office, still unable to deduce a reason for the summons.

"Thanks for coming back," her supervisor said as she motioned Karen to take a seat opposite her. "I wanted to touch base with you to see how you're doing."

"Is anything wrong?" Karen asked nervously, her hands trembling slightly in her lap.

"Well, to be honest, I'm not sure. You haven't seemed like yourself lately."

"Is there a problem with my work?"

"No-o-o-o, not really. But I have noticed that you seem pretty down. You've missed more work over the last four months than I can ever remember. Is everything okay? It's been a long time since I saw you smile."

Karen couldn't deny that her supervisor spoke the truth, only she'd been feeling this way for a lot longer than the past four months. She'd just been better at hiding it before. Not knowing what to say, she looked down at her hands.

Finally, feeling trapped by the silence, she said, "I guess I haven't been feeling much like myself lately. I don't really know what's wrong."

"Karen, you're a valuable employee and someone I'd like to consider a friend. Over the past several months, from where I sit, this hasn't gotten better; it's gotten worse. I'm worried about you. I think maybe it would be good to figure out what's causing you to feel this way."

Are You Depressed?

How do you know if you're depressed? When does sadness become depression? How many "bad days" can a person have in a row and not be considered depressed? How can you tell if how you're feeling is something that's going to get better on its own? These are excellent questions. Before you continue any further into this book, take time to look over the following depression indicators. This is not a scientific tool but rather a way for you to identify contributing conditions in your life.

We will identify two types of indicators: yellow indicators, which signal caution and should be monitored, and red indicators, which signal identified symptoms of depression. Red indicators are certainly important for you to be aware of, but watch for the number of yellow indicators present. Yellows tend to turn into reds over time, if not addressed.

There are certainly all sorts of tools you can use to answer whether or not you're depressed. You can get them online, from your doctor, from books, even from family or friends. The indicators placed in this book are gleaned from experiences at my counseling center, and the diagnostic definitions are from a whole-person point of view. As you look over these indicators, note any that indicate your own feelings.

Yellow indicators can include conditions that have been present in your life for a long time, even a number of years. Red indicators come from the established criteria for clinical depression and, because of the severity, can have a much shorter duration.

Yellow Indicators

- A loss of enjoyment in established activities.
- Feeling restless, tired, or unmotivated at work.
- An increase in irritability or impatience.
- Feeling either "wound up" or "weighed down."
- Feeling overburdened with life and its activities.
- A lack of spiritual peace or well-being.
- Finding relief by controlling aspects of your personal behavior, including consuming liquids or food.
- A fear of expressing strong emotions.
- A constant anxiety or vague fear about the future.
- Feeling unappreciated by others.
- Feeling a sense of martyrdom, as if you are constantly asked to do the work of others.
- Exercising a pattern of impulsive thinking or rash judgments.
- Sexual difficulties or a loss of interest in sexual activities.
- A sense of enjoyment at seeing the discomfort of others.
- Anger at God for how you feel.
- A recurrent pattern of headaches, muscle aches, or body pains.
- Feeling social isolation and distancing yourself from family or friends.
- Feeling trapped during your day by what you have to do.
- Displaying a pattern of pessimistic or critical comments and/or behaviors.
- Feeling like your best days are behind you and the future doesn't hold much promise.
- Feeling "left out" of life.
- Binging on high-calorie foods to feel better.
- Apathetic upon waking about how the day will turn out.
- Feeling it is easier to just do things yourself instead of

wanting to work with others.

- Experiencing recurring gastrointestinal difficulties.
- Feeling trapped inside your body.
- Dreading the thought of family get-togethers or social gatherings.
- Feeling overweight, unattractive, or unlovable.
- Feeling old, discarded, and without value.
- Unmotivated to try new activities, contemplate new ideas, or enter into new relationships.

Red Indicators

- A significant change in appetite, lasting longer than two weeks, resulting in either marked weight loss (if not dieting) or weight gain.
- Recurring disturbances in your sleep patterns for longer than two weeks, resulting in difficulty falling and staying asleep, or sleeping too much.
- Increased agitation or inability to relax, occurring for an extended period of time (longer than two weeks).
- Feelings of fatigue, lethargy, or loss of energy, occurring for an extended period of time (longer than two weeks).
- Feelings of sadness, despondency, despair, loneliness, or worthlessness, ongoing for an extended period of time (longer than two weeks).
- Inability to concentrate, focus, or make decisions, recurring over a period of time (longer than two weeks).
- Recurring thoughts of death or suicide.
- Planning or attempting suicide.

If you answered "yes" to one or more red indicators, do not ignore these signs and just hope they will go away. Talk to a counseling professional who can help you work through these issues in a responsible, thoughtful way.

Moving Forward

It takes courage to honestly evaluate yourself against the criteria listed above, but honesty is the first step toward finding a cure. Through the course of this book, you will find that the whole-person approach to recovery from depression takes into consideration everything from the list above—and provides real answers for relief, from recognizing depression triggers, to identifying faulty coping styles, to understanding clear symptoms of depression.

Now that you better understand what you are facing in terms of recovery, allow me to say again that there is hope. I know because I've been through the valley myself. From my book that chronicles my own journey to wholeness, titled *Becoming Strong Again,* I offer the following words of encouragement:

> *The path leading to…freedom may be the greatest challenge of your life. It will take more than positive thinking, more than reading a book or two, and more than a couple hours of counseling. We are talking about exposing your whole being—the physical, spiritual, and mental—to a lifesaving experience that will help you renew your strength so that you will be able to "soar on wings like eagles…run and not grow weary…walk and not be faint" (Isaiah 40:31). But you may think you barely have the courage, strength, or will to turn the next page…. You must start where you are (and) having just enough strength to turn a page is enough strength to begin with. The good news is you can find healing.*

May you continue to find strength as you work through this book and complete your journey to recovery. There are answers. There is hope.

1

Emotional Currents

We live in an age of depression. It's global and it's increasing. You can't ignore it, and it won't go away without a plan for dealing with it.

Beth wondered, *What is wrong with me?* The worry, never far from the surface of her thoughts, intruded again. But still, Beth had no answer. She felt run down, listless, and unable to generate energy or enthusiasm about anything. She made sure her kids were taken care of and pantomimed her way through a declining number of social functions, but she couldn't remember the last time she could honestly say she felt "good."

Her husband had even commented on her early nights to bed—without him—and her inexplicable lethargy. She wasn't eating, and her clothes had begun to droop on her diminished frame. Even wearing bright colors seemed like a lie. Her smile was a pale echo of its former self, detached from any presumed goodwill.

And it wasn't just her inability to feel joy that frightened Beth. As she'd gone through the motions of cleaning up her youngest son's scraped knee just now, she realized she couldn't even feel bad for him. Empathy had left too, along with joy. Picking him up, kissing his cheek, cleaning his wound and bandaging it, all had been accomplished without the expected emotional attachment. She could display a form of concern, but it was without substance. *What is wrong with me?* she continued to ask herself. *Where did my passion for life go?*

Water Everywhere and Not a Drop to Drink

We live in a society where the opportunities for a vibrant, fulfilling life have never been greater. We have more, we understand more, we control more than ever before. Our choices are staggering. At the start of this new millennium, the future spreads out before us. Yet, depression is on the rise. Research indicates that depression rates have tripled over the last two decades, affecting roughly one in ten Americans.[2] By the year 2020, the World Health Organization estimates depression will become the number-two debilitating disease worldwide, second only to heart disease.

Traditional approaches obviously are not working for many people. The traditional approaches probably haven't worked for you, or else you wouldn't be reading this book, for yourself or for someone you know. You may look around at the flood of choices and view a sea of opportunity available for others, yet wonder why your own joy is cracked and your energy is dried up. If awash in the land of plenty, your life seems a desert, then you, like Beth, have picked up this book hoping to find the answer to that cry of "What's wrong with me?"

The Faces of Depression

As mentioned in the introduction, depression is as individual as the person suffering from it, but it does have some familiar faces. Depression shows itself through a prolonged period of sadness or anxiety. It leaches interest or pleasure out of activities that would normally be enjoyable. Depression alters appetite and sleep patterns. It promotes feelings of guilt, shame, and hopelessness. Depression interferes with the ability to make decisions, to concentrate, to remember things, to focus. It steadily strangles the will to act, producing either a frantic, anxious state or an apathetic lethargy. Depression may lead to recurrent thoughts of suicide and death.

In times past, depression was considered a weakness, suffered by weak people, as evidenced by the higher rate of depression among women.[3]

This chauvinistic, repressive attitude toward depression and its sufferers has been changing, allowing the depressed to come out from under the cloak of shame and seek help for their illness. At the Center for Counseling and Health Resources, we have found, with whole-person treatment, approximately 90 percent of our clients experience long-term recovery. Over the past twenty years of working with depression recovery, we have developed the keys to unlock the secrets of "why people get depressed."

Clients come to our clinic with concerns about anxiety, hopelessness, and feelings of being overwhelmed or increasingly isolated. They do not use the term *depression* to explain their concerns. Either they are fearful of any lingering stigma, or they simply have been unable to place a label on their nameless dread. Some are at the point of suicide, without really knowing why they feel that taking their own life is the only way to end the pain.

Others come to our clinic with difficulties in relationships; they have become moody, irritable, isolated from loved ones, sometimes even abusive. Clients are concerned about their inability to concentrate at work or a lack of productivity that threatens their employment. Sometimes it is not the depressed person who makes contact with us; it is loved ones concerned about that person's behavior. They are concerned about the withdrawal they see or the risky, thrill-seeking behaviors some depressed people will use in an attempt to jolt themselves out of their depression. People have been willing to give up established relationships, jobs, and physical locations as a way to separate themselves from their depression, not realizing the depression will follow them wherever they go.

For some, our clinic is not their first stop. They've gone to their family physician with complaints of vague, chronic physical ailments. They "hurt" here or there. They may be unable to sleep, or they sleep too much. Some are losing too much weight or gaining too much weight. Blood scans, lab work, and physical exams provide no definitive answers. Many times they leave their doctor's office with a prescription for an antidepressant. Some are given a recommendation from their doctor to see a therapist. Occasionally, people will come to our clinic after failed attempts to self-medicate through alcohol or drug use.

However people come to us, often they have already tried several other methods that were unsuccessful in ridding them of depression. Their families have no empathy for their behavior and the apparent lack of results. Those who attempt self-medication through substance abuse have often fractured established relationships, which left them even more isolated than before. I have met with people who are demoralized, confused, and held captive by the debilitating effects of depression, caught in a vicious cycle. They want help. They want answers, and through the whole-person approach, we've been able to supply them.

Just Who Do You Think You Are?

The answers to the question of "Why do I feel this way?" come from a variety of sources. Many important answers come from the first aspect of the whole-person view we refer to as the *emotional self.*

Many people who suffer from depression have lost the ability to absorb and experience joy. Without joy, there is no hope. Without hope, there is no future. Without a future, you question the reason to carry on.

One of the key areas we consider, when assisting clients in recovery from depression during therapy, is how the people feel about themselves. We ask clients in essence, "Tell me who you are and why." If clients are not optimistic and hopeful about their own future, depression can establish a stranglehold. Once established, depression produces the negative self-talk that reinforces feelings of guilt, shame, worthlessness, and helplessness. The person's optimism is drowned in a flood of negative effects from excessive anger, fear, and guilt. Over and over again, we have seen the damage done by these three emotions spilling over their appropriate boundaries and inundating a person's sense of self-worth. In almost every case, this trio of emotions holds the key to depression.

This is not to say that anger, fear, and guilt are completely negative.

If someone treats us poorly, it is natural for us to feel anger over the injustice. If we are threatened in some way, it is appropriate to be fearful. If we have done something clearly wrong, it is healthy for us to feel guilt. This kind of anger helps energize us to protect and defend ourselves. This kind of fear motivates us to quickly seek a solution to our danger. This kind of guilt produces the remorse that allows us to change our behavior.

The emotions of anger, fear, and guilt, in proper proportion, are healthy, appropriate emotions. But, like many things, too much of them can wreak havoc. Left unresolved, these three emotions can eat away at your sense of optimism, hope, and joy.

When Anger Turns Inward

There is a long-established concept that depression is really anger turned inward. That was certainly one of the main causes of Beth's depression. When she first came in for treatment, she expressed concern over her lack of emotions. She felt "grayed out" most of the time, incapable of feeling strong emotions of any kind, especially about her family. She had an overwhelming feeling of guilt that something was "wrong." It was an enormous step just to seek therapy for her depression.

As we worked through the person she was, the person she wanted to be, and the person she thought she should be, Beth experienced her first strong emotional response in a long time. She was surprised when she realized how truly angry she had become. Over the years, Beth had developed a carefully constructed exterior of a calm, reasonable approach to situations. She felt it was important to repress strong emotions in order to project a controlled, quiet response to life. She felt this was expected of her when she was a child, and it seemed especially important for her as she grew older, married, and had a family. With a religious upbringing that valued a woman's "gentle and quiet spirit," Beth purposed to eliminate strong personal feelings from her emotional repertoire. She rejected thoughts of anger, resentment, or jealousy and sought to only express what she determined to be a proper response.

She was thoroughly unprepared for the consequences of this almost-unrecognized decision. The more she denied her feelings of anger, resentment, and jealousy, the more they burrowed deep into her heart. When her husband asked her how she'd spent her day, she rejected the anger she felt at being questioned to give an account of every minute while he'd been gone. When her mother remarked how well her sister's daughter was doing in school, she refused to acknowledge the resentment she felt that her own children struggled with their studies. When a neighbor explained they would be moving soon, she hid her jealousy at their ability to buy a home in a better part of town. Because Beth considered her feelings were inappropriate, she would not acknowledge her true responses to her circumstances. Locked inside, left to fester, they fed her ever-increasing mountain of anger.

The more her anger grew, the less she felt a desire to eat. With her insides churning from anger, food simply did not go down well. The persistent ache of hunger helped cover the distress of her resentment. Without really knowing it, Beth was exchanging hunger for rage. Feelings of hunger were "acceptable," but feelings of anger were not. Along with her depression, Beth had developed the eating disorder anorexia.

Through therapy and a courageous decision not to shrink from what she was learning about herself, Beth worked toward understanding the source of her anger. She realized she'd transferred a perception of perfection from her childhood into her adulthood. Beth realized she was angry that her commitment to being perfect wasn't producing a "perfect" life. She still had struggles. She was angry with her husband, frustrated with her kids, anxious over finances, jealous over the achievements of others, resentful over the demands of family. All of the things she thought she wasn't supposed to feel, she did.

Over the years, Beth developed a pattern of rejecting, instead of accepting and understanding, herself. Intense, unresolved anger was the result. This anger fueled her depression.

Beth learned to accept, understand, and forgive herself. She learned to openly evaluate her way of thinking, realizing the feelings themselves weren't wrong; rather, it was what she chose to do with them that led to difficulty. If her husband asked about her day, she could choose to feel oppressed and interrogated by him, or she could choose to respond with the truth about all of the things, large and small, that made up the hours since he'd left home. Beth realized he wasn't asking her to give an account for the use of her time, but he had a genuine interest in what kind of day his wife and his children experienced. His question wasn't based on accusation but affection.

If her mother remarked on the accomplishments of other members of the family, she could choose to resent any comparison to her own family, or she could choose to rejoice with the rest of her family, realizing that the accomplishments of one person enriched all of the extended family and didn't detract from hers.

Beth learned not to ignore her jealousy over the good fortune of an acquaintance. Instead, she learned to analyze it and reject the pattern of feeling "less than" about herself. She accepted her jealous feeling and used it to remind herself of all of the blessings she had. She used it to motivate her to continue working to accomplish the dreams she set for herself and family.

Beth learned that unresolved, repressed anger was poisoning her optimism for the future, contributing to her depression.

When Fear Takes Hold

Just as anger drains optimism, fear steals hope. Hope is the expectation of a better tomorrow. Fear is the foreboding that there's no such thing. When fear takes hold, the future is not anticipated but dreaded.

When Robert sought counseling, he was practically immobilized by fear. The employee-assistance program at his work had authorized him to attend some therapy sessions due to his dramatic loss of productivity on the job. Over the course of therapy, we looked at Robert's past employment, where he was presently, and where he hoped to be in the future.

Robert shared his deep-seated fear that, at any moment, his "true abilities" would be discovered and he'd be fired.

Three months earlier, Robert learned he was being considered for a major promotion when a senior official reached retirement. Terrified that the scrutiny of the promotion would reveal some weakness in his job performance, Robert sank into a deep depression. Fearful he would be "found out," he worried that instead of obtaining the promotion, he would be fired from his current position. His nightmare became being out of a job and humiliated in front of his long-standing colleagues.

This anxious response to the prospect of a large promotion plummeted Robert into depression and dramatically decreased his job performance. Without realizing it, Robert was attempting to self-sabotage any promotion. He just couldn't seem to get projects done at work anymore. Convinced his every move was being scrutinized for failure, Robert failed to do much of anything at all. He agonized over the slightest decision. His appetite suffered, his sleep suffered, his relationship with his family suffered. He started calling in "sick" and just stayed home. Simply put, Robert didn't feel successful at his current job and certainly not worthy of any promotion.

As we confronted these issues, Robert realized that even as a child and teenager, he'd never felt praiseworthy for any activity he undertook. Unable to please his father, Robert was convinced at an early age that any success he experienced was accidental. Because his father took great pains to explain to Robert what he'd done wrong on any project, Robert developed the impression that the only reason others thought he'd done something well was because they just hadn't looked hard enough. These childhood doubts grew with Robert into adulthood.

One of the things we did with Robert was a review of his job accomplishments. We talked about why he was being considered for the promotion and went over the comments from his last job performance review. We talked about all of the things Robert did that were right.

Then we talked about how Robert viewed the work of others. How he didn't expect perfection in his subordinates, only in himself. He didn't even seem to expect perfection in those above him. We probed the reasons why Robert felt compelled to be so hard on himself.

As Robert was able to squarely and honestly come to terms with the unrealistic expectations of his father, and his own insecurities those expectations had produced, Robert was able to come out of his difficulties at work. He did not receive the promotion but accepted the opportunity his present job offered to devote more time to working on other aspects of his life. Consequently, his productivity at work exceeded his previous performance levels.

Robert is hopeful that another promotion opportunity will present itself in the future. When that time comes, he'll be ready. Robert has moved from fear to hope.

When Guilt Weighs Heavily

Anger drains optimism, fear robs hope, and guilt crushes joy. Joy is an intensely personal pleasure that radiates from the heart and encompasses your entire being. It is exquisite and intimate. Guilt argues against joy, saying you don't deserve such pleasure. Guilt says what you've done or who you are doesn't merit personal happiness.

Cathy was referred to counseling by the courts because of a DUI. She hadn't revealed to the police officer who stopped her that she was on her way to the store for more liquor. Since it was her first offense, Cathy opted to go into treatment for deferred prosecution.

Cathy was an alcoholic; she used alcohol to self-medicate her ongoing depression. She'd been pretty good at hiding it for a long time, but the shame of her alcoholism, combined with her feelings of guilt over her past, created too powerful a combination for Cathy. As her remorse grew, so did the depression. As her depression deepened, so did her alcohol abuse. It was just a matter of time before something terrible happened. Luckily, Cathy was pulled over and arrested before she caused any injury to herself or to someone else.

During the course of her alcohol-abuse treatment, her chemical-dependency counselor recognized Cathy's signs of depression. We have several clients who are able to use both our mental-health and our chemical-dependency services concurrently. Cathy was one of those clients.

As Cathy progressed through the two-year alcohol program, she worked with her mental-health counselor. Together they addressed the reasons for Cathy's feelings of crushing guilt. A rebellious teenager, Cathy became convinced she was the reason for her mother's alcoholism and subsequent death from stroke. Somewhere in her childhood, Cathy tied her mother's drinking with her own failings as a daughter. When she was little, Cathy had tried hard to be "perfect" so her mother wouldn't be so disappointed and have to drink so much. When that hadn't worked, Cathy rebelled as a teenager and went as far from perfect as she could. She stayed out late, engaged in sexual activities, and started her own drinking addiction.

When a classmate became crippled from an alcohol-related automobile accident, Cathy made a decision to clean up her act. She was able to stay away from her more risky behaviors into young adulthood. This turnaround, however, never seemed to make an impression upon her mother. Whenever Cathy was around her mother, her mother would eventually imply how much trouble Cathy had been growing up. Mom's complaints were especially clear when the rent or utility payments were due and Mom expected Cathy to make up for her past behavior by supporting Mom financially. They were both aware Cathy's financial support also made it possible for her mother to continue to drink heavily.

When her mother died suddenly of an alcohol-related stroke, Cathy was unprepared for the unrelenting feelings of guilt her death caused. Instead of putting an end to her feelings of failure as a daughter, her mother's death solidified that guilt. It wasn't long before Cathy began drinking again to numb herself from the pain of that guilt and the severe depression her mother's death had caused.

Once Cathy examined the seeds of her guilt, she understood the truth of her childhood and teenage pain from the perspective of being an adult and was able to forgive herself. Having undergone the bondage of alcoholism herself as an adult, Cathy was also able to empathize with and ultimately forgive her mother. As she did so, her depression lifted and Cathy reexperienced joy in her life.

She went back to community college and obtained a degree as a veterinarian's assistant, realizing that one of the great joys in her life was interacting with animals. During deep times of depression and alcoholism, Cathy had managed to care for and relate to her canine companions. After her treatment for chemical dependency, she moved to the city where her older sister and family lived. Given her past behavior, they were cautious to include Cathy in their lives, but her continued years of sobriety and commitment to her new career have facilitated a renewal of relationship.

Coming Out of the Darkness

One of the remarkable similarities of those who suffer from depression is the common image of darkness they use to describe their depression. They feel burdened, weighed down, and oppressed. In an effort to articulate the unexplainable, the person finds that the overwhelming reality of depression manifests itself in recurring themes of despair and hopelessness. Though each individual may take a different route into that despair, the description of a hollowed-out destination of helplessness is universal.

The stories of Beth, Robert, and Cathy may not be your story. But there may be components of your story in each of theirs. They are presented to demonstrate the wide variety of ways depression can overtake a person and cause emotional lives to become unhinged.

The whole-person approach recognizes these individual paths to depression, its universal signatures, and the reality of individual routes to recovery. In helping each person to identify and work toward his or her own recovery, the whole-person approach acknowledges and addresses the common emotional contributors to depression. We are emotional beings, and no matter the reason for the depression, its expression is through our emotional state.

When a person is depressed, it is vital to discover the emotional roots such as anger, fear, and guilt that firmly lock depression into a person's mind-set. Something is arguing against optimism, hope, and joy. In order to address the emotional component of depression, the root cause must be uncovered, understood, and addressed in a positive, healing way.

Taking a multidimensional approach to recovery increases the rate of success. While there are those sufferers who use medication alone to get a handle on their depression, research shows there is a higher degree of healing when therapy is combined with medication.[4] Therapy or counseling provides individuals with a safe place to talk about feelings and discuss past and current life events that have contributed to who they are now. Therapists can also make suggestions about positive actions people can integrate into their lives. We have found that when the whole-person approach is used, including an understanding of the body and the appropriate use of medication, the rates of recovery are further enhanced.

In the next chapter, we will look at how to experience emotional stability, cognizant of the past, in concert with the present, and mindful of the future.

Courage—An Emotional Key to Recovery

One of the strongest emotional keys to recovery is the courage to identify and acknowledge the source of emotional pain in your life. Many times, the source of this pain is rooted in childhood and may have solidified over the years. It takes courage to look at your pain from a fresh approach. It takes courage to understand the need for change. It takes courage to step out in faith and act.

Write in your journal a statement such as the following: *I am brave enough to understand my pain. I am strong enough to go beyond it.* You can use this statement as written, or you can write one of your own. It needs to be a positive, personal affirmation that articulates bravery and courage for you. Highlight this statement in your journal. Memorize it. Write it down where you'll see it each day. Use it whenever your courage falters. This will be your "moving forward" phrase for chapter 1.

Moving Forward

It's now time to begin to integrate into your own life what you've read. Take a moment to look over this chapter. Reread it, if necessary. From the previous discussions, note at least three areas that express your own feelings. It is not necessary to have every fact line up with your own experience. Choose those ideas or concepts that evoke an emotional response within you.

- Write down and personalize these concepts.
- Use simple words or phrases to write down how you feel about these truths in your life.
- Articulate how these truths motivate you to act.

Be aware that your initial response may be inaction—or paralysis. Try to understand how these truths can motivate you to act. Understanding and integrating truth are key components to action, but action doesn't always come immediately. Remember, this is a process, a journey. As you understand and integrate more and more truths through this process of recovery, you will act.

Use Your Journal to Review Chapter 1

- Moving Forward Phrase: *I am brave enough to understand my pain. I am strong enough to go beyond it.*
- Write how you feel about your own feelings of anger, fear, and guilt. Which is the strongest and why?

- Write down your responses to each of these questions: "What am I angry about?," "What am I afraid of?," "What do I feel guilty over?"
- Answer the following: "When freed from anger, fear, and guilt, I will be able to accomplish (fill in this space with your dreams, desires, and aspirations)."

2

Emotional Equilibrium

Overcoming depression requires a new
paradigm. It can't be solved by the same
circumstances that created it.

Carol ran into the house, trying to get the phone. Too late, she reached to
disengage the answering machine when she heard who it was—her ex-
husband calling to say that he'd be late again on paying his child support.
She folded her arms as if to brace herself as she listened to him weave his
excuse of "too many bills and not enough money."

In the past, Carol would have responded to this news with a helpless
sort of anger. She'd be fearful that any criticism or argument on her part
would mean Jack would just hold the check out longer. He'd done it before, and she'd be afraid he'd do it again. She really needed the money. In
the past, Carol would have said nothing to Jack. Not today.

"Jack, it's Carol. I'm here," she said, picking up the receiver. He seemed
surprised to hear her voice. He began again to rattle off his reasons for not
paying on time before she quietly, but firmly, interrupted him.

"Jack, that's not acceptable. If someone's going to do without this
month, it will have to be the cable company, not your children." There
was silence on the other end of the phone.

"Look," he finally said, "I just called to say I'd be a little late, not that
I wasn't going to pay at all." She could hear the anger in his voice.

Just keep going, she said to herself. *You can do this.*

Intentional Response Versus
Automatic Reaction

Depression is often an emotional reaction to overwhelming circumstances. We may find ourselves in a situation where we feel helpless, so we disengage emotionally. We may feel angry but unable to show it. We may feel frustrated but unsafe to vent it. We may feel burdened but inadequate to bear it. Since we can't seem to express what we're really feeling, we choose to feel nothing at all. The end result we seek is a cessation of the pain. But ignoring pain doesn't make it go away, and minimizing the damage often leads to greater hurt.

What do we do when life feels like it's piling on top of us? Many times, we bury our optimism, our hope, and our joy, then react with fear, anger, or weariness, allowing overwhelming circumstances to knock us flat. This reaction can become so ingrained in our behavior that emotional depression becomes an automatic reaction to life's trials. But depression does not have to be automatic; we can choose to intentionally respond to any circumstance with optimism, hope, and joy.

How is that possible, you ask? Let's look at the case of Carol. Like many single parents, Carol was overwhelmed by raising three children alone. From the outset of her divorce, Carol's ex-husband exacted a penalty for every visitation and every check the court had ordered. It was his way of punishing Carol for having the courage to leave, and his way of maintaining the control he exerted over Carol during their marriage. He quickly set up a pattern of picking up and dropping off the children at the most inconvenient times and places for Carol. When she protested, he made it sound like she didn't want him to have visitation and thus was in violation of the court order. Child-support checks arrived sporadically and rarely on time, but always with an elaborate excuse.

Carol initially sought counseling for her children. It didn't take their counselor long to recommend that Carol come in for herself. Carol was anxious, high strung, and depressed. She needed help switching from an automatic reaction to an intentional response when dealing with the circumstances surrounding her divorce.

The Next Level

Carol needed to find a new response to her ex-husband's repeated offense. Her solution was best stated by Albert Einstein, who said, "You can't solve a problem on the same level that it was created. You have to rise above it to the next level."[5]

The next level above automatic reaction is intentional response. In order to counteract the debilitating effects of anger, fear, and guilt, you need to be intentional in your response to life and its circumstances. You need to deliberately recognize, promote, and sustain optimism, hope, and joy.

What's so joyful about Carol's situation? Through therapeutic support, Carol was able to look at her situation with new eyes. She found optimism in the fact that she had been brave enough to recognize an unhealthy situation in her marriage and end it. If she'd been brave in the past, she could be brave again. Carol found hope in the promise of beginning a new relationship—not with someone else but with herself. Each fresh insight brought hope for future growth and fulfillment as a person. She found joy every day in the smiles of her children.

Carol *found* optimism, hope, and joy. She looked for it and found it. She stopped waiting for these things to come to her and began to actively, intentionally seek happiness. She didn't need to look for trouble from her ex-husband; it had no problem finding her. But Carol took a giant leap forward when she decided to take control over how she responded to the roadblocks from Jack. When she intentionally responded with optimism, hope, and joy, her depression and anxiety lessened.

Recognize, Promote, Sustain

Circumstances that fuel depression are often short lived, but sometimes they must be endured for longer than we'd like. Depression can remain even after the circumstances have subsided. No matter how long you've been depressed, it can be eased by intentionally recognizing, promoting, and sustaining optimism, hope, and joy. It is up to us to create these positive responses; they are available to us every day, no matter what our circumstances.

This observation is not a trite saying but rather an observation made in the depths of one of the cruelest, most horrific situations ever experienced—the Holocaust of Nazi Germany. In his book *Man's Search for Meaning,* Viktor Frankl set about to answer the question of why some people lived through the concentration camps and others did not. He found that it rarely had anything to do with their physical state. Some who were extremely debilitated or ill continued to live, while others who were in much better physical shape died. The difference, he found, was in their attitude to life.

Frankl discovered that in the final analysis, strength for living is found in the ability to choose your attitude, your response to any given situation. The situations he dealt with on a daily basis were deprivation, starvation, physical disease, and beatings. Yet, in the midst of the hell of the concentration camp, he intentionally chose to respond with optimism and hope.

If Viktor Frankl could find those things in the midst of a Nazi concentration camp, each of us has the opportunity to find them in our own situations. It is our responsibility to recognize them, promote them, and sustain them. This is the challenge for the person who is depressed. Let's discuss specific actions you can take to assist you in creating emotional balance.

Positive Self-Talk

Each of us has a set of messages that play over and over in our minds. This internal dialogue, or personal commentary, frames our reactions to life and its circumstances. One of the ways to recognize, promote, and sustain optimism, hope, and joy is to intentionally fill our thoughts with positive self-talk.

Too often, the pattern of self-talk we've developed is negative. We remember the negative things we were told as children by parents, siblings, or teachers. We remember the negative reactions from other children that diminished how we felt about ourselves. Throughout the years, these messages have played over and over in our minds, fueling our feelings of anger, fear, guilt, and hopelessness.

One of the most critical avenues we use in therapy with those suffering from depression is to identify the source of these messages and then work with the person to intentionally "overwrite" them. If a person learned as a child he was worthless, we show him how truly special he is. If while growing up a person learned to expect crises and destructive events, we show her a better way to anticipate the future.

Try the following exercise. Write down some of the negative messages inside your mind that undermine your ability to overcome your depression. Be specific, whenever possible, and include anyone you remember who contributed to that message.

Negative Message   **By Whom**

_____   _____

_____   _____

_____   _____

_____   _____

_____   _____

Now, take a moment to intentionally counteract those negative messages with positive truths in your life. Don't give up if you don't find them quickly. For every negative message there is a positive truth that will override the weight of despair. These truths always exist; keep looking until you find them.

Positive Response

_____

_____

_____

You may have a negative message that replays in your head every time you make a mistake. As a child you have been told, "You'll never amount to anything" or "You can't do anything right." When you make a mistake—and you will because we all do—you can choose to overwrite that message with a positive one, such as "I choose to accept and grow from my mistake" or "As I learn from my mistakes, I am becoming a better person." During this exercise, mistakes become opportunities to replace negative views of who you are with positive options for personal advancement.

Positive self-talk is not self-deception. It is not mentally looking at circumstances with eyes that see only what you want to see. Rather, positive self-talk is about recognizing the truth, in situations and in yourself. One of the fundamental truths is that you will make mistakes. To expect perfection in yourself or anyone else is unrealistic. To expect no difficulties in life, whether through your own actions or sheer circumstances, is also unrealistic.

When negative events or mistakes happen, positive self-talk seeks to bring the positive out of the negative to help you do better, go further, or just keep moving forward. The practice of positive self-talk is often the process that allows you to discover the obscured optimism, hope, and joy in any given situation.

Navigating the Flow of Moods

Michael was a truly amazing individual, incredibly intelligent and articulate. He came to us for help as a teenager, after his best friend died through suicide. With that death, Michael buried both his friend and his optimism. When Michael's mood was consistently one of pessimism and biting sarcasm, his family realized he hadn't just buried his own optimism; Michael had declared war on theirs.

No matter how hard they tried to get along with him, Michael awoke each day chained to the same bad mood from the day before. After enduring his sour moods for several months, Michael's parents insisted that he get counseling. Their insistence deepened Michael's anger. He needed that anger. He wanted that anger.

When he first arrived at the Center, he was surly to everyone at the reception desk. He was both hostile and apathetic to his counselor. He made no effort to alter his mood; rather, he reveled in it. He wore his bad mood as an act of defiance to a world where the sun still rose even though his friend was dead and Michael was in such pain.

Through counseling, Michael learned it was okay to be angry. The person he was really mad at was his friend who had abandoned him through suicide. He didn't think it was right to be angry at his dead friend, so he was angry at everyone else. Anger also gave Michael a way to channel his pain without dealing with it. As his anger subsided, Michael found a safe place to come to grips with the pain of his loss. The more he dealt with the pain, the less need he had for his anger.

Once Michael understood the source of his anger and depression, his perpetual bad mood began to lift. He started to return smiles and greet those at the front desk. Instead of speaking in monosyllables, he responded pleasantly to polite inquires about his day. He opened up, ever so slightly, about upcoming events. Hope and positive anticipation about the future returned. The depression he'd descended into lifted, and Michael returned to a healthier balance of good versus bad moods. He still experiences lousy moods occasionally, like all of us, but they no lon-ger last for weeks at a time.

One of the skills we teach clients is mood mastery, or how to choose their mood. All of us have a profusion of moods at our disposal at any given time. So often we choose negative moods simply because we've formed a habit of submitting to their strong presence. We've allowed them to take shortcuts to the forefront of our moods.

Mood mastery is akin to choosing your attitude. Mood and attitude are linked; they are interrelated but separate. Mood is how we are feeling; attitude is how we respond to the mood. Choosing our attitude, our re-sponse to the mood, is one way we can actively achieve mastery over any mood. No matter what mood we initially experience, our attitude can either reinforce that mood or cause us to choose another.

Let's be clear. Choosing a mood is not about reacting to an event or circumstance. Things happen and each of us will have a natural reaction, such as surprise or anxiety, that may be similar to the way anyone else might react. It is what happens next that falls under the category of choos-ing our mood. After our initial reaction, we have the opportunity to re-view that reaction, then intentionally respond with a continuation of that reaction or respond with one of our other mood choices.

Here's a common, everyday example: We're in our car on the way to work. Maybe we're running a little bit late. All of a sudden, the car next to us swerves into our lane, cutting us off. Our reaction is probably one of shock and surprise. It may even be anger. It's upsetting when we feel endangered or surprised by the irresponsible action of another driver. What happens next, however, is a choice.

We can choose to take a deep breath and back off the bumper of that car, realizing it'd probably be a good idea to give a little bit more room between that driver and ourselves. In other words, we can choose to re-spond intelligently.

We can also choose to respond angrily. An extreme example of this response has the name *road rage*. It begins when the actions, real or perceived, of another driver produces an angry, aggressive response. Even if it doesn't go as far as road rage, we can still respond by using that event to fuel a bad mood. We can choose to react to that event by remaining angry about it long after the fact.

If an event such as getting cut off on the roadway can produce a day-ruining reaction, it's not surprising that other, more serious or traumatic events can lead to a sustained bad mood lasting months or even years. Once people understand this concept, we work to support them in expanding the moods they choose from in responding to life.

Choosing a good mood promotes optimism, hope, and joy. A good mood allows you to experience these life-affirming emotions. When you are experiencing depression, you must work at promoting the choice of a good mood. It can be hard work. A good mood won't come naturally, while unconstructive moods will. Pessimism, negativity, sarcasm, hostility, even apathy flow freely when you are depressed. To overcome depression, you must turn the flow of this negative tide and strive, even if it seems like you're paddling against a strong current, to promote optimism, hope, and joy.

Your perceptions can be another challenge. We have often found that depressed people do not perceive their responses to life to be negative. They view apathy as a "neutral" response. They have spent so much time being negative that it feels to them like the absence of emotion. If the person does not rant or rave, or shout, or become verbally aggressive, she may not recognize that her chosen response to life is negative or bitter.

One of the ways we help people understand the impact of their moods is to ask them to examine a variety of situations in their lives. We ask about family, jobs, hobbies, recreation, and general interests, even events of the day. The person in a perpetually bad mood will rarely have something good to say about any of these. If there is a positive comment, it is usually expressed with a qualifying statement or a series of negatives attached to it. For example, a person may comment that his job is going all right but immediately add that the busy season hasn't hit yet and if it's going all right now, with it being so slow, all hell's sure to break loose once production gets up and running.

After we have gone through this exercise, we point out to our clients the common threads of pessimism we see in their responses. It is remarkable how many times depressed people are unaware that they respond in such negative ways. This exercise helps the depressed person to recognize his or her own pattern of harmful thinking.

Next, we specifically ask the person to respond in each area with positive—and only positive—comments. Sometimes, there is a long silence as the person realizes she truly can't think of anything positive to say. The good news is that persistent negativism is only voluntary. In other words, people can choose to intentionally look for the good and to respond from a positive point of view, even if they've chosen to be negative in the past. The longer they have been negative, the more difficult and "unnatural" a positive viewpoint will seem. But change can and does happen.

Runaway Thought Train

Jill suffered a devastating anxiety attack. She had been depressed for months over her upcoming fiftieth birthday. Instead of being a celebration of a half-century of life, Jill dreaded the date. She forbade her family from making "a fuss." She refused to go out with friends as the date approached. She was emotionally distant and began to complain of a variety of physical ailments. Instead of engaging in social events and her normal routine of volunteering, Jill spent months going from doctor to doctor, unable to find out why she was feeling so bad. The weekend after she wound up in the emergency room at our local hospital, Jill called to see a counselor.

Together they worked on the reasons for her depression and subsequent anxiety attack. During their time together, the counselor noticed that Jill talked a great deal, almost nonstop. Once she got started on a topic, Jill would keep right on going. One thought led to another, and another, and another. Often, the thought three or four steps down the line had only a marginal connection to the first. This runaway thought pattern helped contribute to Jill's depression and anxiety attack.

Jill was concerned about turning fifty. She thought about all of the conditions and health problems she'd heard about in those over fifty, from cancer, osteoporosis, and menopause to Alzheimer's. As she dreaded her approaching birthday, she convinced herself that being fifty automatically meant a loss of health and vitality. On the night of her panic attack, the spiral of her thoughts led her to believe that common indigestion was actually a heart attack. The more she worried, the more adrenaline surged through her system and the faster her heart raced.

The faster her heart beat, the more she was aware of it. It seemed abnormally fast and beating erratically. Jill remembered hearing a radio commercial about the signs of a heart attack, and sure enough, she suddenly found herself experiencing each one—rapid, erratic heart rate; shortness of breath; lightheadedness; tingling in her extremities. These symptoms, of course, are also present during anxiety or panic attacks.

The humiliation of creating such a crisis in her family caused her to worry she was losing control over her mental processes. This fear of losing mental control prompted her to come in for counseling, something she had never considered in the past. Her counselor coached Jill to "slow down" and practice thought containment.

Many times, emotional depression and its companion, anxiety, can be brought under control when the depressed person learns to contain his or her thoughts without letting them escalate into predetermined catastrophes. Jill had convinced herself that her fiftieth birthday would bring nothing but problems, so it did.

It is part of the human condition that negative thoughts seem to flow easier than logical and more positive ones. An overactive brain can take a small incident and inflate it into a major crisis. If this pattern is repeated often enough, the person becomes swept away in this mental torrent, unable to find the footholds needed to return to the solid ground of common sense and reality. When the flow of thoughts slows down, the person is able to better realize the truth and maintain a grip on the probabilities.

If a person is naturally pessimistic, inclined toward runaway thoughts, depression is often the result. The person who feels powerless to control his thoughts assumes that the worst that can happen soon will. This focus on disaster does not allow the person to keep optimism, hope, or joy in his sights for very long, if at all. Negative self-talk and the grim atmosphere of a foul mood fuel this fatalistic mental spiral.

Getting to the Root of Hidden Anger

For Carol, Michael, and Jill, anger penetrated from the core of their depression. For Carol, it was anger toward her ex-husband for continuing to exert control over her life, via the children. For Michael, it was anger toward his friend for taking his own life. And for Jill, it was anger toward the inevitable health problems she associated with the aging process. Yet although these three people are now well aware of the anger underneath it all, their anger was once muddied or masked—behind Carol's grin-and-bear-it acceptance of *un*acceptable behavior, behind Michael's stinging sarcasm, and behind Jill's obsessive thinking.

In fact, hidden anger can manifest itself in any number of ways, many of which may surprise you:

- Procrastination in the completion of tasks, especially ones you don't like or want to do. What do you put off? Work deadlines? Phone calls? Laundry? Grocery shopping? Car maintenance? Going to the doctor? Paying the bills?
- Habitual lateness. Are you late everywhere you go, or are there patterns to it? Always late to work but early for engagements with family and friends? Or is it just the opposite?

- Sarcasm, cynicism, or flippancy. Within what context do you typically make sarcastic, cynical, or flippant remarks? Is it only with certain people or only within a certain context? In other words, is your hidden anger tied to a certain person, in terms of what she brings out in you, or is it more general, tied more to how you feel in specific situations as opposed to whom you are with?
- Overpoliteness, constant cheerfulness (fake), attitude of "grin and bear it" but internally resenting it. As with sarcasm, cynicism, or flippancy, is your overpoliteness or constant cheerfulness tied to a particular person, or is it dependent on the circumstances you are in?
- Frequent sighing. You may not even realize you are doing this, so make a note to be mindful of how frequently you sigh, and within what context. Again, is it usually around a certain person, or is it more specific to an activity (i.e., work task), thought (i.e., all your to-dos), or situation (i.e., dealing with a conflict at work or home)?
- Smiling while hurting. As with frequent sighing, this may not be something you are particularly aware of. Next time you notice yourself smiling, though, check in with your head and heart. Does your expression match what you're thinking and feeling inside?
- Overcontrolled monotone speaking voice. This is not only a means of hiding anger but subsequently any number of other feelings that are not allowed expression. In other words, masking a negative feeling, such as anger, inevitably trains you to mask positive feelings as well, such as surprise, excitement, and joy.
- Frequent disturbing or frightening dreams. The keyword here is *frequent*. We all have bad dreams and nightmares

now and then. But if they are persistent and you wake feeling scared and unrested, anger could be at the root.

- Difficulty in getting to sleep or staying asleep. Thoughts going around in your head keep you awake. This is a pretty common symptom of any number of underlying mental, emotional, or physical issues. It should probably only be considered a symptom of hidden anger if other symptoms of hidden anger are present.

- Boredom, apathy, loss of interest in things you are usually enthusiastic about (depression from internalized anger). These responses, though they may seem just the opposite of hidden anger underneath, may be your body's means of dealing with these negative feelings in the only way it knows how—by numbing them. Rather than feeling anger, your body seems to prefer to feel nothing at all.

- Slowing down of movements, especially when doing things you don't want to do. This is another form of procrastination. Instead of tackling a task with enthusiasm and the intent of finishing it, you may subconsciously (or even consciously) slow down a task that you resent doing in the first place, from folding the laundry at home to drafting an e-mail at work.

- Getting tired more easily than usual. Again, this can be a symptom of any number of underlying issues, so it is to be taken into consideration only within the context of other symptoms of hidden anger.

- Excessive irritability over trifles. Road rage is a perfect example. Granted, there are times when other people's driving habits can be dangerous and warrant a strong reaction. But when you "lose it" on the guy in front of you for missing the light or forgetting to turn on his blinker, the anger you're feeling was already there, just waiting for an opportunity to erupt. The same is true of other minor incidents throughout any given day, from spilling your coffee to having trouble with your Internet connection.

- Facial tics, spasmodic foot movements, habitual fist clenching, and similar repeated physical acts done unintentionally. Again, these are things you may or may not even be aware of. As with all the other symptoms of hidden anger on this list, simply be open to noticing their presence and mindful of when they occur.

If any of these ring true for you, understand these are not behaviors to be cursed or vilified. Instead, consider them welcome warning signs that anger may be hiding in plain sight. The key is getting to the root of the anger, which may or may not relate to a specific event. In fact, your anger is most likely tied to beliefs and relationships that span your lifetime.

Unfulfilled Expectations

Whether we realize it or not, we all have an underlying set of expectations for life—some fulfilled, others not. That's life, plain and simple. The problem lies in the difficulty some of us have in *accepting* unfulfilled expectations. These beliefs about how life is supposed to be are so ingrained in us that the possibility of failing to meet said expectations is too much to bear. What we've been promised isn't delivered, and that makes us mad!

Anger stemming from unfilled expectations can probably be traced back to one or more of the following falsehoods we carry through life:

- I need to be perfect to be happy.
- When I am upset, it is the responsibility of others to comfort me.
- When others harm me, it is intentional.
- When I harm others, it is a mistake.

- The more intense my pain or discomfort, the less the rules apply to me.
- I deserve to be taken care of by others.
- Others must carry my burdens for me.
- If I am angry, no one else has the right to be.
- No one works harder than I do.
- The people now in my life must make up for the pain caused by the people in my past.
- I am always taken advantage of by others.
- I am supposed to deny my own needs for the needs of others.

Of course, these are not beliefs that we pull out of thin air. In most cases, they originate with family members who pass down these falsehoods, including the behaviors that manifest and reinforce them. Beyond family, we tend to enter into relationships in which our belief systems are validated, as painful and maddening as they may be.

Keeping Score

Actions speak louder than words, and in the case of anger, your action of holding on to a grudge or a memory trumps any words you frame as forgiveness that you do not mean. This is not to suggest you are intentionally misleading someone into believing you have forgiven her. It means only that sometimes the *expectation* of forgiveness is so overwhelming that you do not give your underlying feelings the validation they need and deserve. As a result, the forgiveness you may *want* to give is held hostage by thoughts that won't go away:

- That person has never apologized or shown any remorse.
- I'm not going to let that happen to me again.
- It still makes me mad to think about it.
- What happened to me was so unfair I can't get over it.
- I'm not going to let that person off the hook.

So how do you release yourself from the grip of thoughts tying you to a grudge? It can be as simple as observing the underlying thoughts (above), then choosing new thoughts that reinforce a healthier move in the right direction:

- It's not worth the pain to keep thinking about it.
- That person is out of my life now, so what's the use?
- I've grown up and moved on with my life.
- We were kids when that happened, and we've both grown up.
- I've come to accept that's just the way this person is, and she's never going to change.

Granted, these new thoughts may feel foreign to the language of self-talk you have become accustomed to expressing about this person. Thus, mindful attention is key—to what you're thinking and what you *want* to think in the practical pursuit of genuine forgiveness.

Stress

Typically, any pressure to perform we feel in our daily lives generates from an external source, or so it would seem. At home and at work, you are constantly being held responsible for meeting the expectations of others—physically and emotionally. However, the majority of the time, these are expectations for which *you* have made *yourself* responsible. In most cases, these are probably activities you want to be responsible for, but no doubt there are times and circumstances under which you say yes when you would prefer to say no. Actually, "preference" suggests you could go either way. In fact, saying no is often critical to maintenance of your overall well-being—emotionally, environmentally, relationally, physically, and spiritually.

The next time you are feeling overwhelmed by the pressure to perform, control, or "fix" something—for yourself or for someone else—weigh the possibility of simply letting go:

- To "let go" does not mean to stop caring; it means I can't do it for someone else.
- To "let go" is not to cut myself off; it's the realization that I can't control another person.
- To "let go" is not to enable poor behavior or choices, but to allow learning from natural consequences.
- To "let go" is to admit powerlessness, which means the outcome is not in my hands.
- To "let go" is not to care for but to care about.
- To "let go" is not to fix but to be supportive.
- To "let go" is not to judge but to allow another to be a human being.
- To "let go" is not to be in the middle arranging all of the outcomes but to allow others to affect their own destinies.
- To "let go" is not to be protective; it's to permit another to face reality.
- To "let go" is not to deny but to accept.
- To "let go" is not to nag, scold, or argue but instead to search out my own shortcomings and correct them.
- To "let go" is not to adjust everything to my desires but to take each day as it comes and cherish myself in it.
- To "let go" is not to regret the past but to grow and live for the future.
- To "let go" is to fear less and to love more.

At the Center, this list has proven effective for motivating positive change in clients, so consider bookmarking this page and referring to it often.

Life Is Unfair

When something bad happens, it is natural to be angry and to fear the prospect of it happening again. More often than not, though, the true danger lies in the anger itself. The closer we keep it, the more we confuse the anger with ourselves. It becomes our identity, through which we cast ourselves as victims in any number of subsequent circumstances throughout our lives.

If you suspect you are holding on to anger related to any specific event in your past, ask yourself these questions:

- As I think back on what happened to me, was there anything I could have done to avoid or prevent it?
- Knowing what I know now, how will this knowledge affect my life and choices today?
- How has holding on to anger about those experiences helped or harmed me?
- Based on what I've learned about myself through this experience, how will I use this knowledge positively going forward?

Unresolved Relationships

Any one of the areas referenced above—relative to hidden anger—could, and probably does, include an unresolved relationship. From your past or in your present, anger associated with someone you know could be fueling the fire of anger.

Who taught you the falsehoods at the root of your unfulfilled expectations?

Whose wrongs are you keeping score of, or who is keeping score of *yours*?

Who guilts you into doing things you do not want to do?

Who hurt you in the past, a pain you may be imposing on new relationships?

Whether you are aware of it or not, you probably have an underlying desire to resolve your relationships with these people. In some cases, this may mean a face-to-face encounter is in order. In other cases, it may mean simply "doing the work" on your own, recognizing the equal roles you both played in the relationship and choosing to move on from there.

The Compounding of Countermeasures

Depression is a countermeasure for anger, as we choose to feel nothing over feeling the unrelenting pain of anger. This issue is challenging enough to treat on its own. However, in some cases, depression is just one of numerous ways we deal with anger. In fact, depression may also be accompanied by

- addictions
- alcoholism
- eating disorders
- frigidity
- gambling
- hypochondria
- irresponsibility
- irritability
- judgmentalism
- lying
- overcommitment
- panic or anxiety
- perfectionism
- self-aggrandizement
- sexual promiscuity
- smoking
- substance abuse
- vicarious living
- workaholism

Again, it is normal to have more than one countermeasure associated with anger. So if you recognize more than one of these behaviors in yourself, choose gratitude for the knowledge as opposed to regretting time lost to hidden anger.

Sustaining Optimism, Hope, and Joy: Keys to Emotional Equilibrium

It is vital for your emotional equilibrium that you counterbalance anger, fear, and guilt with optimism, hope, and joy. The promise of the whole-person approach means that the healthy aspects of a person can support the weaker characteristics until the whole person is strong and well.

Intellectual, relational, physical, and spiritual aspects of your life can also assist you in sustaining the life-affirming emotions of optimism, hope, and joy. We will discuss each of these aspects of the whole-person in later chapters, but the following exercises are offered to acquaint you with their principles.

Intellectual Support

To support emotional balance, be aware of the information you are feeding to your mind. Try reading a positive, uplifting book, and *intentionally* set aside time in your day to fill yourself up intellectually with constructive, encouraging messages. Reading this book can be a way to intellectually support a healthy emotional life. Be aware of what you are reading and listening to, and seek to counter the negative input we all get as a part of our day with positive influences.

Relational Support

Think of a person you really enjoy talking to, someone who makes you feel good about yourself or someone who's just fun to be around. It could be a family member, a coworker, a teller at the bank, or anyone who brings a smile to your day. *Intentionally* plan this week to spend time with that person, even if it's just for a moment or two. Make the effort to verbalize your appreciation for his or her positive presence in your day.

Physical Support

Physical activity is a wonderful way of promoting emotional health. Engage in some mild exercise this week. Take a walk around the neighborhood. Stroll through a city park. The goal is twofold: to get your body moving, and to allow you to focus on something other than yourself and your surroundings. Take a little time when you're in the neighborhood and greet your neighbors. Stop while you're at the park and watch someone playing with his dog, or cheer at a Little League game. *Intentionally* open up your focus to include the broader world around you.

Spiritual Support

Take some time to nourish your spirit. If you are a member of a religious organization, make sure to attend services this week. If you are not, listen to some religious or meditative music. Spend time in quiet reflection, meditation, or prayer. *Intentionally* engage in an activity that replenishes and reconnects your spirit.

Moving Forward

Each of these actions may seem like a small step. They may even seem unachievable, given the way you feel. Please, do them anyway. If you are emotionally out of sync, you can't rely on how you're feeling to determine what you do. Each of these actions, done intentionally, will help you in two ways: (1) they will assist you in focusing on optimism, hope, and joy; and (2) they will reinforce the truth that you can intentionally respond to life and its circumstances. Like Viktor Frankl, you can *choose*. Today, choose optimism, hope, and joy.

As you record in your journal this process toward overcoming depression, you will find that aspects of this book will impact you differently as you gain new insights to their truths. It is extremely valuable to be able to articulate what you are feeling as you uncover and acknowledge why you feel the way you do now. It will be helpful to review your insights and moments of clarity, especially during times of discouragement.

Allow yourself to become your own encourager. Identify what things hinder and help you, and write those initiators down. Take a moment right now to use your journal. Don't be afraid to express strong, intense emotions. Allow them to come out through what you write. If you feel overwhelmed, visualize the strong feelings flowing out of you through whatever you're writing with and anchoring on to the pages of your journal. Now they are recorded and accessible to you if you ever feel the need to express yourself. Your written words can be a conduit for those feelings, allowing you to experience them without becoming overwhelmed the next time.

In your journal, write a statement similar to this one: *Today, I choose to focus on optimism, hope, and joy.* Memorize it. Write it where you can see it. This is your "moving forward" phrase for chapter 2.

We've talked about the inner conditions we create for ourselves through our emotional states. Next, we'll look at how the outside environment affects our ability to overcome depression.

Use Your Journal to Review Chapter 2

- Write down some of the negative messages that undermine your ability to overcome your depression. Include the names of anyone you remember who contributed to that message.
- Write a positive truth to counterbalance each negative message.
- Write down what situations or comments initiate negative self-talk.
- Write down conditions that help or hinder you to be your own encourager. (Be sure to include those that help, and don't overly focus on those that hinder.)
- Moving Forward Phrase: *Today, I choose to focus on optimism, hope, and joy.* Memorize it.

3

The Pressures of Life

Depression is the opposite of peace; it is the
foundation for anxiety.

Jim hated going to the grocery store. It seemed like every time he turned
around, they had changed the layout. He didn't know where to go to find
what he wanted. A lot of the time, he didn't even know what he wanted.
Deciding meant making choices, and lately even that took too much
energy.

Did he want a red, blue, or yellow toothbrush? Regular or diet or
caffeine-free or caffeine-free diet soda? He could get sandwich bags in
fifty or one hundred fifty, fold top or zipper top. Ground meat in extra
lean, lean, or regular. Milk in whole, 2 percent, 1 percent, skim, fat-free,
or enriched. Twelve types of eggs, thirty types of margarine, and fifty
kinds of cheese. Kleenex came in small square boxes or medium boxes or
large rectangular ones. They could be scented or unscented, colored or
not, with lotion or not. There were one hundred count or two hundred
count. Toilet paper in single- or double-ply, plain or quilted.

Jim just stood in the middle of cart traffic, trying to make a decision
in an entire aisle of sliced bread. Should he get plain white or honey wheat
or seven grain or multigrain? Should he get the larger loaf for $2.99 or go
for the smaller, cheaper kind on sale for $1.99?

And when he'd overcome all of those choices and survived to make
his way up to the counter, he had to decide on the regular line, the express

line, or the self-checkout line. Did he want paper or plastic or both? Was he going to use cash, credit, or debit? Did he want to use any coupons? Did he want cash back? Did he need any help out? Should they put the groceries in the front seat, backseat, or trunk?

It was all staggering.

Outer Assault

It is one thing to make the mental decision to recognize, promote, and sustain optimism, hope, and joy. It's another thing to keep a calm determination to do so when there's a storm raging around you. A turbulent lifestyle can quickly overpower our emotional equilibrium. For many of us, the way we conduct our lives severely impairs our best intentions. After making the decision to intentionally seek out optimism, hope, and joy, you may find it difficult to maintain this commitment amid the pressures of everyday life. As you cultivate the positive, you must also assess the areas in your life that may be working against your desire to overcome depression. How you're *living* may be just as important as how you're *feeling*.

The Pace of Life

A hurried, fast-paced life has a way of draining our natural resiliency. Bit by bit, particle by particle, detail by detail, the sheer weight of the lives we lead can wear us down, leaving us feeling inadequate and devastated. Life, and its pace, can rob us of peace. When peace leaves, depression takes up residence.

Jim came for counseling after that pivotal trip to the grocery store. His wife had sent him to pick up a few things. After all, he was just sitting in his chair doing nothing, and she was busy with the laundry. After shaming him into compliance, Jim agreed to go, even though he just wanted to sit and do nothing. It took him two hours to get a bag of groceries worth

$27.89. By the time he got to his car, he just sat there with tears coursing down his cheeks because he couldn't even go to the store successfully. Defeated, he was terrified he'd gotten all of the wrong things and spent too much money. God knows he'd already spent too much time.

Time is a precious commodity in our fast-paced society. If you want to insult another person, just call him or her "slow." We pack more and more activities into our day until our schedules are calculated to the minute in order to get it all done. Accomplishing one task isn't satisfying when seven others are lined up to take its place. When the speed of life overtakes the substance of our activities, we are on a crash course for depression. Like the proverbial rodent in the wire wheel, we spin and spin, going faster and faster, but getting nowhere. When this truth finally dawns on us, we break down and stop moving altogether.

Jim had spent his entire life spinning faster and faster. He'd gotten a job at twelve and had worked since then, sometimes holding down two jobs. After he'd married, Jim got a job with a local trucking firm, running the warehouse. It was a job that demanded intense concentration, extraordinary commitment, and an on-call capacity anytime the delivery schedule demanded. The job gave Jim a sense of momentum with direction and purpose. When a national firm bought the company and closed the local distribution center in favor of one in San Francisco, hundreds of miles away, Jim was suddenly without a job. At fifty-three, he felt old by industry standards but knew he had many years before retirement.

Jim sank into a deep depression after repeated attempts to find work failed. After spending years at the heart of whirlwind activity, Jim could barely get motivated to leave his chair. Adrift, without a purpose, Jim found it harder and harder to get up day after day. With each rejection, he felt older and more useless. His energy dwindled, and his hope drained away.

Pat, like Jim, also felt she needed to be busy to prove her self-worth. While his activity had centered around his work, hers centered around her home. Pat took seriously the phrase "A woman's work is never done."

She never took time to slow down. On the contrary, Pat used every moment of every waking hour in order to get done all of the things she felt were vitally important. Completing tasks took on a higher priority than nourishing relationships. Pat spun a frantic web of endless activity, defying anyone to get close to her.

The faster Pat moved, the more momentum she built up. After years of this pattern, Pat found it impossible to relax. The more she did, the faster she worked. The faster she worked, the more she did—moving the bar of "productivity" up farther and farther. The force of her productivity began to sweep up other tasks. Soon, she was caught up in household chores, her children's school, community involvement, church activities, and neighborhood programs. Oftentimes, the only view her family had of Pat was as she headed out the door to the next important event.

Pat became bummed out, frustrated, anxious, and exhausted. She became bitter and resentful of others. After all, she was spending all of her time on important tasks, while others had all the "fun." She began to complain of not feeling well and, one by one, dropped out of activities, often with little or no warning. She refused to return phone calls and withdrew from her family even further.

If you wind up a mechanical toy and let it go, that energy is released in a flurry of activity. The more you wind up the toy, the faster it goes. But what happens when you wind the toy up too far? It breaks and doesn't move at all. That's what depression does to those who go spinning through life. Eventually, the pace winds them up too far, and they break down. The result is depression and emotional exhaustion.

Many of us go through life doing things for the wrong reasons. Jim thought if he wasn't moving and working, he wasn't worth anything. Pat thought that because she wasn't "working," she had to fill up her life with worthwhile things to have personal worth. Both looked for activity to give purpose to their lives. When Jim lost his job and stopped working, he lost his purpose. When Pat reached emotional exhaustion and stopped doing, she lost her sense of value.

This pace of life was one both Jim and Pat created for themselves. The answer to overcoming their depression was not in returning to their previous activities. We helped each of them to evaluate their activities, which revealed to Jim and Pat the underlying patterns that contributed to their depression.

The Patterns of Life

Pat grew up feeling as if it was a sin to say no. If someone needed help, she gave it. If there was a job to be done, she did it. If she saw a need, she took care of it. Her favorite fairy tale growing up was "The Little Red Hen." Over the years, she developed a pattern of feeling superior to others through her efforts and hard work. She looked down on those who did not work as hard as she did, who didn't accomplish as much. Because she looked down on those who did *less,* this motivated her even further to do *more.* Her sense of value and worth came from what she *did* as opposed to who she *was.*

Jim grew up the middle of three brothers. While the older brother excelled in school and the younger brother excelled in sports, Jim excelled in neither. College was not an option for someone from Jim's lower-middle-class family. Instead, he found his worth in work. While his brothers could boast about academics or athletics, Jim could pride himself on how well his job was going.

Never considered overly attractive by girls in high school, Jim assumed that the main reason his wife married him was because of his "stability" and well-paying job. He took pride in being a good provider for his family. When he lost his job and had difficulty finding another, Jim's long-held belief in his own mediocrity propelled him into depression.

Both Jim and Pat had negative patterns of thinking about their own lives. These patterns were based on a flawed understanding of the source of personal value and true worth. As long as circumstances cooperated, they were able to ignore the weaknesses in their personal foundations, even as those patterns continued to erode optimistic views of their lives. Eventually, however, both Jim and Pat crashed.

The Predicaments of Life

The pace of life can exhaust us. The patterns of life can undercut us. Unexpected dilemmas, such as the loss of a job, the illness or death of a loved one, a financial crisis, the necessity of a move, or personal health problems, can erode our emotional equilibrium. Difficulties such as these attack our sense of security and can rob us of happiness. Even the most carefully constructed life comes with surprises. Life happens.

When Peter lost his wife of twenty-three years to colon cancer, he thought he could work his way out of his grief and depression. With their two children grown and away from the house, Peter worked longer and longer hours to avoid going home. He got scared when he realized that even when he was home, the house seemed "empty." He felt empty, a year after his wife's death.

Peter turned to treatment after an emotional conversation with his daughter. She told him she felt like both of her parents were dead, but one just wasn't buried yet. Peter had dismissed the idea of counseling, thinking it was for those who couldn't solve their own problems. It was an enormous step for him to admit he needed help dealing with the grief of his wife's death and the depression it brought. Peter was humbled to realize how he could be knocked off balance by life. He'd always thought that bad things happened to "other people." Peter was unprepared when bad things happened to him.

The Perceptions of Life

When someone experiences a significant loss, depression can occur. Peter lost his wife and, for a while, his emotional bearings. His depression resulted from the loss of something tangible, the presence of a loved one. This kind of loss can lead to grief, depression, and crushing sadness.

Another source of depression comes from frustration and despair. It isn't based on the loss of something, but on the absence of something that was never there in the first place. It is depression based on the *perception* of loss. It is depression based on the death of expectation.

The philosophy that a half-empty glass is an empty glass is one of the most destructive perceptions of life. This is the idea that if the glass is not filled to the top, brimming over, it might as well be empty. It is an "all or nothing" perception that flies in the face of reality. No one's glass is ever truly filled all of the time. Life simply doesn't operate that way.

As the saying goes, the healthy perception is to view the glass as having fullness. For those who are depressed, they don't see half-empty; they see completely empty. Some will rage because the glass never seems to be full. Others will despair because they are convinced they aren't worthy of even a half-empty glass. Others will quietly accept the fact that the glass will never be full for them. They look at the glass and see what isn't there, instead of what is. They focus on what is absent instead of on what is present.

The Pluralities of Life

In today's tech-intensive world, we invest increasing amounts of ourselves online—our time, our energy, our identities. But for all the time and effort we put into our virtual lives, how much do they really reflect the truth? In all probability, what you share on your social networks is reality skewed through the ability to only post the best of yourself, or at least what you believe to be your best. It is because we have so much invested in our online personas—which we seemingly control, at least more so than in real life—that the prospect of disconnecting can feel devastating.

In my book *#Hooked: The Pitfalls of Media, Technology, and Social*

Networking, I cite a study of "disconnect anxiety." In it, participants described the following feelings when unable to connect via the Internet, e-mail, social networks, texting, chat, and other online activities:

- feeling lost
- having only half a voice
- disoriented
- panic
- tense
- empty
- dazed
- inadequate
- getting behind in the flow of information
- loss of freedom

Paradoxically, we all suffer from plenty of anxiety when we *are* connected (or doing our best to be). Maybe there's a slow Internet connection or no connection at all! Maybe we're overwhelmed with a multitude of social networks we're intent on updating on a daily basis. Or maybe we're suffering from information overload, struggling to stay on top of every development—from world news to the latest from our Facebook friends' news stream.

In other words, at any given moment throughout your day, the desire to connect online may be a source of anxiety. Even the conscious decision to voluntarily disconnect can be anxiety ridden, making you certain you're going to miss something or, worse, that your "friends" and "followers" are going to forget you.

If you suspect you may have an unhealthy level of anxiety associated with your online activity, or lack thereof, consider the following criteria used to determine nonchemical addiction:

Importance: How important has it become to your sense of self and the way you live your life? You can determine importance not only by how much you're doing it but also by how much you're not doing other things. Priority equals importance.

Reward response: Does doing it make you feel better and more in control? Does not doing it make you feel worse? Doing things you enjoy makes you feel better. Avoiding things you dislike can make you feel better, at least initially. There is a positive payoff to all this activity that can obscure the activities' negative consequences.

Prevalence: Do you find yourself doing it more often and for longer periods of time than you originally planned? If you feel compelled to say "Just a little bit more" all the time, you're carving out more and more space in your life for these activities. The question becomes, in order to carve out this time, to what else are you taking the knife?

Cessation: Do you feel anxious or uncomfortable if you cannot do it or if you just think about not doing it? One way to gauge how important these things have become to you is to consider doing without them. The higher the level of panic and pain you anticipate, the stronger the hold they have over you.

Disruption: Has doing it disrupted your life and your relationships, causing interpersonal or personal conflicts over what you're doing?

Reverting: Do you often say to yourself you're going to do something different but then turn around and keep doing the same thing—or doing it even more? Before you know it, you're right back to doing what you did, and more.

As someone who embraces and loves all the latest and greatest in new media and technology, I am not immune to the near-constant call of connection to the virtual world. That's why I must be constantly mindful of the extent of my online activity, frequently checking in with myself to be sure I'm maintaining a healthy balance of living online and off!

Moving Forward

It is difficult to recognize, promote, and sustain optimism, hope, and joy on the inside when life isn't measuring up on the outside. You feel as if you're running and running but getting nowhere. It seems you keep smacking into the patterns of your past that complicate your present. Every time you get back up on your feet, it seems life throws you another curve. The glass always seems to come up empty for you and not for others. In the midst of all of that disappointment, how can you find and keep joy?

The answer is in taking back control, as much as is possible, of the outside environment of your life. Each aspect of life—the pace, the patterns, the predicaments, the perceptions—can gather so much momentum on their own that it's easy to forget how much control we really do have over our own lives.

As we discussed in the previous chapter, we can choose our attitudes. In a great many instances, we also choose our activities. Either we allow our activities and our circumstances to carry us along, or we take control of the direction our lives are going.

Take a moment to examine what you do each day. What are your major, and minor, activities? In your journal, divide a page into four columns. In the first column, write "Activity." In the second column, write "Filling" (representing activities that you find fulfilling and energizing), and in the third, write "Draining" (representing activities that tire you and drain you of hope). Entitle the last column "Overall." Choose the first six activities that come to mind. Write those in the left hand column. Then evaluate what elements of those activities are *filling* and what are *draining.* Some of the activities may contain both filling and draining elements. In the right-hand column, indicate whether, on the whole, that activity fills you with energy and joy of life, or drains you of hope and optimism. You will use this chart later on.

Your "moving forward" phrase for this chapter is the following: *I choose to view life as fulfilling.* As you work on these positive "moving forward" statements, you will be reprogramming your mind to dwell on the positive. This is not a gimmick or an optional activity. Actively, intentionally use these statements, or those you have written for yourself, to reintroduce hope and a sense of what is possible back into your life.

In the next chapter, we will evaluate more life activities, such as where you are putting your time and energy, and whether those activities are filling you up emotionally or wearing you down. We'll evaluate why you engage in certain activities and what they say about the patterns you've developed over the years. We'll examine which activities fortify you through the predicaments in life, or weaken your ability to ride out life's storms.

The environment you create for yourself is vital in overcoming your depression. It's time to intentionally plan what you do on the outside, to fortify who you need to be on the inside to overcome depression.

Use Your Journal to Review Chapter 3

- Moving Forward Phrase: *I choose to view life as fulfilling.*
- Choose six activities, and determine whether each is a draining activity or a filling activity. As some activities may contain both draining and filling elements, decide whether each activity is draining or filling overall.

4

The Purpose-Filled Life

Living a life of purpose is one of the greatest
defenses against depression.

Carmen stepped into the classroom and asked, "Pam, I'm headed off to
lunch. You about ready?"

"I'll just be a few minutes. Meet you down there," Pam responded,
shuffling through a stack of papers on her desk. She wanted to make sure
everything was set when her sixth-grade class returned from lunch and
recess. True to her word, after a few minutes, Pam was satisfied and headed
toward the lunchroom. As she backed out into the hall to shut the door, she
took one last look at her classroom. *Her classroom*—that felt so good.

At forty-six years old, Pam was a first-year teacher. She'd started
out her career as a social worker but, after almost twenty years, realized
her job was wearing her down. She saw the kids after they were already
in trouble and in "the system." She felt her ability to help kids at that
point was limited, and the frustration of the job became a drag on her
optimism and her motivation. She had dreaded going to work each day.

After taking an extended vacation, Pam realized she did not wish to
return. Instead, she decided to go back to school for her teaching certifi-
cate. She wanted to work with older-elementary kids. She wanted to
make a difference in their lives earlier than she'd been able to before. She
had served twenty years as a social worker and figured, after schooling,
she'd have just about as much time as a teacher.

Pam loved being a teacher. She took everything she'd learned—both the good and the bad—from her social-work experience and was using it to be the best teacher she could be. It wasn't so much that she was starting over as that she was expanding.

This job is so rewarding, Pam thought as she caught the smells from the kitchen, *it almost makes up for cafeteria food.*

Taking Stock

> "God grant me the serenity to accept the things I cannot change, courage to change the things I can, and wisdom to know the difference."[6]

To paraphrase the famous Serenity Prayer, it is so important to recognize those things in our lives that we can change and those things we can't. While there may be a great deal in your own life that you cannot change, you may be surprised at how many things you can. One of the keys to overcoming depression is to honestly and realistically evaluate your life, then develop a plan to accept those things that are unchangeable and a plan to change those that are possible. This requires taking stock of your life. Just as a storekeeper takes an inventory of all that he has, it is wise for us to make a tangible list of our physical, mental, and spiritual assets and liabilities. Make a list in your journal of all your responsibilities; write down what you want to do or be in addition to what you have already done or become, and consider what needs to happen (or stop happening) to fulfill your hopes and aspirations.

You may be reluctant to do this exercise for fear that it will make you even more depressed. But the objective of taking stock is not to create an inventory of all the things that are wrong with your life. Rather, taking stock will help to categorize the changeable and unchangeable things in your life to intentionally move forward, out of depression.

Too often, we live our lives feeling like spectators instead of active participants with the power to choose our own course. We get caught up in life's flow, whether good, bad, or neutral. Wherever the currents take us, we go. It's as if we are on autopilot, but depression happens when our autopilot gets stuck in a negative descent. Unless we take intentional action, chances are that circumstances won't force a change to the positive.

In other words, if you go along waiting for some "thing," some event to alter the course of your depression, you'll probably be disappointed. It's time to take control and look at where you are in your life. It's time to actively and intentionally participate in the course of your life.

Changing the Pace

Over the years, it is possible for the activities and responsibilities of life to layer one on top of another. The combined weight of all of these activities and responsibilities can be crushing. One of the first things to do in taking stock of your life is to look at what you are doing. Look back at your journal at the six activities you wrote down after the last chapter. At the end of this chapter, you'll be asked to expand on that list. You'll be directed to think of the things you are doing daily, weekly, monthly, and otherwise periodically.

For your journaling, you'll be asked to think about your reasons for engaging in each of your activities. What are those reasons? Are they still valid today? Are your reasons for engaging in each activity the same today as they were when you started? Have the reasons changed? Have you? This is an intentional, purposeful look at the activities that fill up your life, including family, work, recreational, religious, and community. It is possible, over time, for an activity to become unhinged from its original reason. If your life is filled with too many activities separated from abiding reasons for doing them, then it is possible for you to feel that your life is not making a difference, that what you are doing and how hard you are working make little difference. Life can seem busy and burdensome, yet without purpose. This outlook can be a major factor in environmental causes of depression.

As you look over your activities and how you are filling your life, what you are looking for is twofold: the first is the number of activities, and the second is the overall effect those activities have on your life. Depression can occur when the amount of activities are either too great or too small. If you are engaged in too many activities, your life can become a blur of motion without any real substance, and depression can result. Benjamin Franklin said, "Do not confuse motion with action." If you are engaged in too few worthwhile activities, and have isolated and insulated yourself from outside relationships, this motion without action can result in depression.

You should also look at patterns that develop for your activities. If, for example, your *filling* activities only happen periodically and your *draining* activities happen more frequently, your activities are out of balance and are contributing to your depression. If, on the other hand, you find it difficult to come up with many activities in your life, this inactivity has actually become an "activity" in your life, and a draining one at that.

Depression can occur when your activities are out of balance in the following ways:

- You have too many activities, and the sum of them outweighs their individual value. When you've got too many things going collectively, you're too busy to enjoy any of them individually.
- You have many activities but too few worthwhile ones. When the sum of your activities is draining, the draining ones interfere with the worthwhile ones.
- You have too few activities in your life. When your biggest activity is inactivity, you rob yourself of the stimulation and engagement of purpose and people.

You may find that you are simply too busy. If so, you need to evaluate which activities to continue and which activities to let go. Or perhaps you have isolated yourself from meaningful, worthwhile activities and will need to stretch and expand yourself, even if it means giving up some activities so you'll have time to integrate more worthwhile ones into your schedule. Intentionally changing the pace of your life can help you move forward in the recovery from depression. By evaluating the substance of your activities, you can make informed choices about which ones to add, which ones to support, and which ones to let go.

Understanding the Patterns

As we discussed in the last chapter, lifelong patterns can significantly impact your ability to get off autopilot and take control of your activities.

If you have developed a pattern of tying self-worth to activity, you may find it difficult to let go of some of the things you are doing. If you have developed a pattern of believing in your own incompetence, taking on new activities may frighten you with their potential for failure. If you have developed a pattern of being afraid of making mistakes, an honest appraisal of why you are engaging in an activity may be uncomfortable because of needed changes an examination might reveal.

In order to continue taking stock of your life, you will need to press on. Don't let any initial hesitation stop you from being honest with yourself. Be mindful of these life patterns, but don't allow them to thwart your efforts to analyze your actions and make necessary changes. As you continue to work through this book, you will gain a greater understanding of the sources of these patterns. For now, it is enough to know that these life patterns exist and can alter your chance for contentment if not confronted and changed.

In your journal, write down some of your life patterns. These will emerge as you think about your reasons for doing, or not doing, activities. They will be the source of your internal motivations and your secret fears. Please be honest about these patterns. They may come prepackaged with convenient excuses that you will need to unwrap to discover the truth.

For example, you may be involved in your community for the outward reason of "civic responsibility," when in actuality you chose this activity because of the power it gives you. It may be power and influence you are after, more so than the good of the community.

You may be working at your job because you "need the money," when in truth you are working at that job because you are too frightened to look for another line of work, one that might be more financially or personally rewarding.

These primary, underlying reasons are either the source of great purpose and fulfillment in your life, or they are a main source of your frustration, disillusionment, and depression. It is vital that you be able to look at these motivations, and look at yourself, as you seek to find the peace asked for in the Serenity Prayer. These are your foundations, and you will need to determine which ones to keep and which ones to replace with something stronger.

As you look at each of the activities you've written down (and be sure to include the times that you are habitually inactive), take time to truly examine why you are engaged in that activity. Allow this honest evaluation of your time to help uncover some of your own entrenched life patterns. You may discover that many of your significant life patterns are negative in nature. Many of these will stem from your childhood experiences and will be examined in the next chapter on relationships.

Understanding that you have developed negative life patterns does not diminish you as a person. On the contrary, this new understanding will allow you to assume more control over the patterns and change them if necessary.

Altering Perceptions

Your life patterns are the result of your perception, or view of life, and what you believed would happen. These are often forged in childhood. Once you understand your personal life patterns, you will be better able to discover certain perceptions and expectations that led you to either negative or positive actions. If your life patterns are framed in negativity, you can be sure your perceptions and expectations were also negative. The more negative your perceptions and expectations become, the greater they support any negative life patterns.

Another way to think of these perceptions is as filters, through which you view the events of your life. Some people, who seem perennially happy, are considered to view life through "rose-colored glasses." Their filters are weighted on the side of the positive. In depression, life is viewed through "gray-colored glasses." Life appears negative, oppressive, filled with shadows.

In overcoming depression, one of the main areas you may need to change is the way you view life. For example, if you believe that life consistently treats you unfairly, then the inevitable ups and downs of life are filtered through that perception. Up times seem imaginary and are enjoyed, if at all, with suspicion, while times of disappointment are considered normal or par for the course. Every down time that happens strengthens the idea that it's just the way your life is.

If you have the perception that your life is supposed to *always* be smooth sailing, the inevitable downs can cause great anxiety. Down times are not put into a proper perspective because you don't consider them to be legitimate in your life. Down times are supposed to happen to other people, but not to you. If you are unprepared to deal with these down times, confusion, frustration, and depression can result.

If you have the perception that you don't really deserve to be happy, you will filter the events of your life to make sure you aren't content. Good things will be met with suspicion, and bad things will be welcomed as old friends.

If you have the perception that the only way for you to be safe is to be in control, you will have a heightened sense of anxiety over life events. Since people are rarely in total control over their environment, and never in control of other people, this perception leaves a persistent, nagging feeling of insecurity. This perpetual sense of unease can lead to anxiety and depression.

Perceptions are so powerful that they can become engines for self-fulfilling prophecy. Mary had the perception that she didn't deserve to be happy. She grew up in a household where blame was constantly conveyed. Usually the blame fell on her, and she developed the view that happiness was only for those who never did anything wrong. Sensitive to her every flaw, Mary didn't believe she deserved to be happy.

True to this perception, when Mary got older, she chose to be in a relationship with a man who treated her poorly. Instead of waiting for and seeking out someone who could truly love her, Mary settled for someone who, for a variety of reasons, merely needed her. Rather than feel guilty at being happy, she chose instead the familiarity of chronic unhappiness. It was hardly surprising when she entered treatment at the Center for depression after her eighteen-year-marriage ended in divorce.

Mary's perception that she didn't deserve to be happy sprang from a life pattern developed in childhood, based on internalizing blame for the bad in any situation. Her pattern of life growing up was one of blame and accusation in her family. From this, guilt grew and crowded out any expectation of personal happiness for Mary. She married a man who didn't love her, who treated her without respect because she didn't feel worthy of anything else. When the marriage ended, Mary felt even worse. She knew her marriage wasn't the greatest but sank into a deep depression when even that ended in failure. One of the most significant things we do at the Center is to help restore a person's sense of self-worth apart from oppressive guilt. Mary learned she wasn't a bad person or a failure in life. Even though her marriage was over, Mary began to live life—her life— for the first time.

By acknowledging negative perceptions, you can move forward toward a view of life that is neither unrealistically rosy nor unrelentingly gray. Acknowledging your pace, patterns, and perceptions allows you to control them, altering them to support your optimism, hope, and joy, even when life throws you a curve.

The Storms of Life

Life does not always flow smoothly. Circumstances can alter the most carefully constructed life. Unlike the pace, patterns, and perceptions of life, predicaments are not something we can actively change. It is not possible to completely shield ourselves from disappointment, despair, or death. Traumatic events will be part of each of our lives. That we cannot change. What we can change, however, is our response to those traumatic events. In addition, by making changes in the areas of pace, pattern, and perception, we can be better prepared when the inevitable storms of life occur.

If the fundamental foundation for our lives is based on negativity, we will have little support when bad things happen. If our lives are tottering and out of balance, a significant traumatic event can cause our optimism and hope to come tumbling down. It could be a death or an illness, an empty nest, a change in job, the loss of a relationship, or the strain of aging. When the pace, patterns, and perceptions of life combine to throw our emotional equilibrium off balance, then depression can be the resulting crash.

Be a Brick House

A familiar childhood fairy tale is "The Three Little Pigs." Each pig builds his house out of a different material in order to protect himself from the huffing and puffing of the big, bad wolf. The house made out of straw is destroyed, as is the house made out of sticks. The house that survives is the one made of brick. Even though it takes more time and work, the brick house is seen as worth the effort because it provides lasting protection.

Examining your life patterns and making positive changes require your time and effort, but doing so is like building your personal house out of brick. By making changes, and understanding the need for those changes, you are constructing—brick by brick—a strong, resilient house that can stand up to the huffing and puffing of life's storms. While reconstructing your house with brick, you'll also need to remove some of the inferior materials you've used to patch weak spots. Remember, this restructuring process will not diminish you but make you stronger. Consider this process of taking stock of your life as your own personal remodeling project.

As you spend time journaling the activities you are currently engaged in, and whether or not those activities are *filling* or *draining*, the key to these activities is in finding a healthy balance for you. This will depend upon your personality, your stage in life, and your unchangeable life factors. Depending upon your personality, you may be the sort of person who simply needs more time to be inactive or still than others seem to need. Or you may be the kind of person who is energized by activity and interaction.

While it is possible to alter your personality to some degree, each of us has individual traits that we need to factor into our activities. We are not alike, and the same activity or activity level will affect us differently. (Some of the many positive outcomes from overcoming depression can be a deeper understanding of your personality, insight into what characteristics you want to enhance and strengthen, and knowledge of what aspects you are ready to change or let go.)

In balancing your activities, be aware of any that are negative and occur frequently. These are activities you will want to evaluate for change. Pam found that her job was becoming a significant negative in her life and made a decision to change careers. Even though this was a major change, it was feasible for Pam to do, given her age and situation.

But what do you do if the significant, recurring drain in your life is not something you can change? What if, for example, you are the caregiver for a parent or terminally ill child or spouse? This is a reality you cannot change, but it may be possible to alter that activity to introduce more help. Significantly draining activities are usually those in which we have assumed major responsibility. They can be especially draining when we must deal with those activities or situations alone. But is that really the case? It may be possible for you to ask for help. One of the perceptions you may need to change is that you must do the job alone.

Julie came to us while caring for her terminally ill mother. She was stressed, overwhelmed, and burned out. Julie was also extremely angry with the other members of her family, including her father, who seemed incapable of assisting Julie in the caregiving responsibilities. According to Julie's perception, her family members were uncaring, incompetent, and content to watch her work herself to the bone without providing help. Trying to care for her mother and her own family became a constant strain on Julie, and she began to break down.

Julie came in focused on her family members and why they weren't caring for her mother. Instead, we focused on why *she* was. Over the years, Julie had developed a martyr or savior complex within the family. Highly negative and critical of others, Julie convinced herself that she was the most capable person in the family. She created a pattern of promoting her feelings of self-worth by taking on draining activities without asking for help. Through looking honestly at the course of her mother's illness, Julie was able to see how other family members had tried to become involved and that she had rebuffed their efforts as ineffective or insufficient. The more she pushed people away and the worse her mother's condition became, the greater the burden she shouldered.

Julie was able to realize this treatment of her family was a life pattern. She had always considered herself to be the only responsible child— the savior—of the family. Julie was able to understand that her need to care for her mother—to martyr herself—was her way of exerting control over the pain her mother's illness caused her. She learned it did not make her less of a person to realize she needed help. Julie recognized that her insistence on total control over her mother's care was detrimental to the acceptance and grieving process of the other members of the family.

About a year after Julie began counseling, her mother died. But during that year, caring for her dying mother became a family-building activity. Instead of being an exclusively draining activity, her mother's dying also took on filling aspects as Julie was able to reestablish fractured relationships with the rest of her family. Julie still grieved the loss of her mother, but through the process she gained a new perspective on her family and herself.

It may not be possible for you to completely eliminate a significant draining activity in your life, but it is possible to evaluate that activity and intentionally purpose to find ways to make that activity include *filling* moments. Sometimes the filling aspects of a draining activity come from the relationships you build with others as you go through that activity. Don't overlook the silver lining of friendships in the storm clouds of life.

As you continue to evaluate your list of activities, look for filling activities that occur infrequently. Determine whether or not you are able to increase the frequency of these activities. Is there any way to engage in a similar activity that will also be personally filling? You may take an art class once a week that is personally rewarding but are not able to devote the time for another class. You can, however, get outside and walk through your neighborhood, letting nature's canvas inspire you for that one class you can take. It is amazing how such small changes can add optimism, hope, and joy to your life. Moving forward doesn't always happen in giant leaps. Sometimes, the most significant progress is made in a series of small steps.

Moving Forward

Making changes in your life requires a certain level of creativity. Creativity requires a certain level of optimism. If you find it difficult to be optimistic and creative, consider working with a caring professional, friend, or spiritual counselor. Oftentimes, when the process of evaluating your life activities is done with the help of others, their vantage points offer perspectives you aren't able to see. Borrow their optimism, hope, and joy until you are able to generate those refreshing, renewing feelings on your own.

Take time now, in your journal, to explore what activities you are engaged in and why. Using these activities as a guide, think about your reasons for spending your time as you do. What do your activities say about you as a person? What are you hoping to accomplish through these activities? Are these activities how you really want to spend your time, or are they dictated by someone else? Do you feel pressure to engage in these activities, or do you do so willingly? These questions will lead you toward hidden patterns and perceptions. Every time you uncover one of these patterns or perceptions, write it down. Look at it. Examine how it may be shaping the pace of your life and your ability to weather the predicaments of life without letting them depress you. Make sure to be alert to positive patterns and perceptions that support your optimism, hope, and joy.

Now, using a new piece of paper, write down "Five Things I Know About My Life." Record anything that you have uncovered as a perception or pattern. What did you write down? Were these statements positive or negative? Look closely at the negative ones. Where did they come from? When did you start believing them? Who told you those were true?

If you haven't written down any positive things, take some time and think of at least two. Hang on to the positive ones, and use them as additional "moving forward" phrases for this chapter. Write them down where you can see them. Keep them at the forefront of your mind. Allow them to refresh you.

Hopefully, you were able to come up with some positive statements about your life to use as your "moving forward" phrases. If not, consider using this one: *My life is worth a strong foundation of optimism, hope and joy.*

Remember, the phrases you are writing down and memorizing are meant to help you move forward. These ideas and concepts are to propel you onward, to support you in your continuing journey of recovery, and to assist you in living a life filled with meaning and purpose.

When the reasons we do things come from negative, destructive patterns and perceptions, life no longer seems worth the effort. Often the breeding ground for our negative pace, patterns, and perceptions of life comes from our families as we were growing up. They dash our optimism, hope, and joy and complicate our recovery from depression. In the next chapter, we will look at the role past, present, and future relationships play in overcoming depression.

Use Your Journal to Review Chapter 4

- Moving Forward Phrase: *My life is worth a strong foundation of optimism, hope, and joy.*
- In this chapter you'll be doing quite a bit of work in your journal, really looking at what you fill your day with, and why. For some of you, it will be enough to catalog your activities and begin to make decisions about their true value in your life. It may require greater time to investigate the reasons behind your decisions and trace them back to life patterns and learned perceptions. For some, this is a journey that is best accomplished with the help of a counselor.
- Leave yourself plenty of space in your journal so you can come back and add insight and information to this chapter as you continue reading and working through the book.
- Do, however, continue to work through this process of taking stock of your life. The goal is to make progress, not necessarily to complete this assignment before moving on through the rest of this book.

5

Family Dynamics

Dysfunction leads to oppression, which leads to depression.

"I don't know who I am," Kevin said softly to himself. It was as if he had amnesia, except he realized he hadn't forgotten his past; he had just never really known who he is. Kevin thought about his childhood and teenage years and realized he had never felt fully present or actively engaged. It seemed to him that he was always moving at the edges of life.

When Kevin was a small child, he was Danny's younger brother. Danny was older and smarter and stronger. Danny was larger than life— at least larger than Kevin's life. When he was in junior high, he'd relished his intentional ability to seem invisible; it had been an excruciatingly awkward time when anonymity was often a blessing.

In high school, Kevin blended in as one of a group of guys, unre- markable individually but finding solidity in numbers. Adrift after high school, he never finished college and instead found his identity in manag- ing a fast-food restaurant. Adulthood meant recognition as a uniform and a nametag, but not as an individual.

When Kevin got married, he became Sheryl's husband, she being much more outgoing than he. It was the same after the kids came. His identity expanded to Heidi's and Steven's father. But the older they got, the less they seemed to need him.

As he thought about it, Kevin realized his sense of self always came as a corollary to someone else.

"If I'm going to get over this," he said, "I've got to learn who I am."

Core Relationships

Recovery from depression is a journey, and as in any journey, one step leads to the next. We have looked at how important it is to cultivate an attitude of optimism, hope, and joy as a safeguard against the squalls and storms of life. We've explored how our environment and lifestyle choices can either positively or adversely affect our emotional equilibrium. We've looked at the role that pace, patterns, and perceptions have in our ability to cope with the predicaments in life. Through the last chapter, you've begun to take an in-depth look at some of the patterns and perceptions in your own life.

In this chapter, we'll look at the role of relationships in forming these patterns and perceptions. Normally, the key to how we view life origi-nates in our childhood and formative years. Our families framed our own understanding of who we are and our belief in who we can be. Our parents and siblings set the stage for our current relationships with family, friends, and acquaintances.

Families give us our first lessons about ourselves. We learn to view ourselves through the eyes of those we love and with whom we have rela-tionship. Each person in the family tells us more about ourselves through our mutual interaction. The family itself, as an entity, tells us about our place in this world. These lessons, over time and into adulthood, can fade from our memory, but they continue to run in the background of our lives, often without conscious notice.

How our families perceived us, and the words they spoke to and about us, continue to echo in our self-view as the background noise of our lives, and we consequently repeat the patterns and perceptions that we held in their presence. Their comments whisper to us in the quiet of the night and in the moments of despair. What they said becomes extremely important to our current ability to recognize, promote, and sustain optimism, hope, and joy. If these learned patterns and perceptions are negative or debilitating in nature, they undercut our commitment to think and act positively.

Learned Invisibility

When Kevin came to us, it wasn't because of any major trauma in his life. Yes, his kids were teenagers, but they were doing fairly well with the adolescent transition. He'd settled into a comfortable relationship with Sheryl, and his job was stable. Yet, Kevin was battling a profound depression. He didn't understand why and couldn't see any way out of it. What began as a couple of sessions of counseling through his employee-assistance program at work became a yearlong journey of discovery. This journey would take him from his childhood, through his young adulthood, and into early middle age. Through this journey, Kevin became acquainted with someone he'd never really taken time to know before—Kevin.

In Kevin's household, there was only room for one dominant personality—his mother. She ran the household, her husband, and her children. Opinionated and vocal, her personality permeated the entire house. She did not allow others to express strong feelings, either positive or negative. She was the conductor of all thoughts, feelings, and opinions in the house. Others could express themselves but only at her direction. Kevin's older brother, Danny, waged a constant battle, chafing against these restrictions. As he watched the fallout between this clash of wills, Kevin determined never to be put in that position. Unlike Danny, Kevin was afraid of his mother.

Over the years, Kevin developed a pattern of withdrawing into himself, becoming "invisible" around his mother, and forcing himself to merge his identity and personality into hers. What she liked, he liked.

What she didn't, he didn't. If he had a different feeling or reaction, he did not express it. He came to understand that this was the tactic used by his father, who seemed to "click" himself off whenever Kevin's mother entered the room, retreating to the television or the newspaper.

Kevin continued this pattern by aligning himself with other, more dominant personalities. He allowed himself to take his sense of identity from other people in his life. It seemed safer that way.

This pattern produced a perception that Kevin was unremarkable, that he really didn't have many thoughts or opinions, that he was a follower and not a leader. Kevin became the person who would be chosen by a leader, but not chosen to lead. By the time he reached middle age, Kevin was no longer content to be considered unremarkable. He longed for others to see him as a person of value and worth. But he was afraid it was too late. Kevin was afraid he'd spent his whole life hiding in the shadows.

To overcome his depression, Kevin needed to understand that it was safe to come out of hiding.

Learned Helplessness

Janet grew up in a family of victims. Nothing bad that ever happened in her family was considered to be their fault. If a bill was late, the post office was to blame. If the car broke down, the mechanic was to blame. If a job was lost, the economy was to blame. Employers were never fair. Workers never did the job right. Teachers were biased. Neighbors were mean.

"Incompetent and uncaring" physicians were the reason Janet decided to try mental-health counseling. The doctors didn't understand what she was going through. They didn't listen to her complaints. They minimized her symptoms and misdiagnosed her problems. She couldn't get better because others were not doing their part to figure out and fix what was wrong with her.

Janet developed a pattern of externalizing blame for every bad occurrence in her life. She perceived herself as powerless to control the bad things that happened. All she could do was complain at the injustices that befell her. Janet had learned that she was not responsible, that she was helpless, a victim of callous disregard and circumstances. As such, she felt totally out of control when it came to her depression. She went from professional to professional, trying to find a "fix." She felt even more victimized when she found fault with every solution offered. Janet came to counseling after her doctor suggested she might benefit from it in conjunction with the medication she'd been prescribed.

In order to overcome her depression, Janet needed to recognize how much control she really did have over her own life.

Learned Worthlessness

Colleen's father let his opinion be known early and often that she'd never amount to much. No matter what Colleen accomplished in life, it was never enough. If she did well in school, she still wasn't smart enough. If she excelled in sports, she still wasn't fast enough. If she did well in business, she still wasn't savvy enough. It was never enough because Colleen was never enough. Colleen was not Collin, for that would have been Colleen's name if she had been a boy. But she wasn't, and her father had never gotten over it. Frankly, he didn't have much use for girls; he already had too many of them and he'd been assured by his wife that Colleen was going to be Collin. He'd pretty much written her off from birth as an extra girl.

Colleen, however, had not written him off. She'd developed a pattern of demanding perfection in herself. Only through perfection could she hope to obtain her father's blessing. She was sure his approval dangled out there, just out of her reach, as she stubbornly refused to believe he had no intention of giving it to her.

Colleen's father died without ever telling her he was proud of her. As an adult, Colleen thought she could rationalize this loss and move on, but she remained stuck. She began to lose interest in her job and activities.

More and more, she isolated herself in her apartment. With the door of his approval permanently closed, Colleen found it difficult to stave off the crushing feeling of her own worthlessness.

In order to overcome her depression, Colleen needed to understand she could supply her own approval and feelings of worth.

Learned Impatience

At fifty-two years of age, Ray was used to controlling his life. As the head of a department in a major company, Ray gave orders and expected immediate results. He told people how high to jump, and they did. Those who didn't measure up to Ray's level of expectation didn't last long. Ray was finally at a place in his life when he felt like everything was working the way it was supposed to—his way.

Then he suffered a major heart attack. After the initial convalescence, Ray was devastated by his body's lack of responsiveness. He wasn't healing as well or as quickly as he expected. He tired more easily. Ray felt betrayed by his body, and each physical setback pushed him closer to the edge of depression; he was afraid that if he didn't recover his physical strength soon, he never would.

Ray had developed a pattern of pushing through life's challenges, using his intellectual and physical strength. These were things he'd always counted on. Make a decision. Get the job done. Go on to the next. Fix whatever was broken and move on. The reality of Ray's recuperation was not living up to this perception. The inconsistency was deeply disturbing.

In order to overcome his depression, Ray needed to understand that some things in life simply couldn't be ordered or forced.

Learned Responses

Families act as incubators for learned responses to life, both positive and negative. While positive responses support our emotional equilibrium, negative responses can bog us down, making it difficult to remain afloat under the tide of life. In order to work through the causes of your depression, it is time for you to think intentionally about how the responses to life you learned while growing up may be hindering you now.

As you think about your family, what did you learn about life? These can be responses you've acknowledged, or those you observed but never really articulated. Often the most negative responses to life are those unspoken truths of your family. Some have called it the family secrets. It is important in your recovery to examine these negative responses so they can be properly evaluated and placed in the context of your life. At the end of this chapter, you'll take time to write down these unspoken truths in your journal.

Emotional Abuse

Sadly, some of the most destructive family patterns and perceptions come from abusive situations. The devastation of physical and/or sexual abuse is overt and terrible. Less visible but still harmful is the emotional abuse that can result from imperfect family relationships. (For an in-depth look at emotional abuse, please see my book *Healing the Scars of Emotional Abuse* in the Resource List at the end of this book.) So much emotional abuse is caused by the negative, destructive messages communicated to children while growing up.

Family members can perpetuate emotional abuse without recognizing the amount of harm being done. The intentions of adults in a family may not be to pass along negative responses to their children, yet through their own inability to control these responses, they set up negative patterns for their children to follow. As children follow these patterns, the negative perceptions that accompany them become grounded in their lives.

Without ever being told, children develop a working model for life based upon the suspicion, insecurity, perfectionism, self-centeredness, frustration, or oppressive behavior of their parents. This model produces feelings of worthlessness, helplessness, and hopelessness, all of which suffocate optimism, hope, and joy.

You may have a background where abuse of this type, or worse, was evident in your family. It will not be difficult for you to pinpoint how these negative experiences have impacted your ability to balance yourself emotionally. Or you may look back at your childhood and conclude your family can't be a source of your depression because you didn't have an abusive experience. Take the time, however, to really examine the patterns you learned from your family.

As much as parents try to minimize the damage done to their children through their own mistakes and faulty behaviors, it is not possible to completely eliminate negative influences. A careless comment or unkind remark can be enough to plant in a child's mind a seed that grows into a poor perception.

This is not a search through your past to assign blame, but rather a mature look at the learned responses from your family to discover those that might be contributing to the strength and longevity of your depression. It is so important for you to be able to identify the burdens from past relationships that may be slowing down your rate of recovery. Once you discover these hindrances, you will be equipped to develop a plan for moving forward. (If you have Internet access, go to www.aplaceofhope.com for a special audio download on "Healing the Scars of Emotional Abuse." This message of hope offers insights into how to identify emotional abuse in your own life and how to move beyond it.)

Take some time to write in your journal about these family responses. Use these statements as a starting point for writing down your recollections: "The good things my family taught me about life," "The negative things my family taught me about life," "The good things my family taught me about myself," "The negative things my family taught me about myself." It is important for you to remember the good and positive responses to life you learned growing up. Most likely, your experiences with your family will be a mixed bag of good and bad, positive and negative, uplifting and deflating. While you want to be cognizant of the negative, don't forget to highlight positive things you learned. For each negative life response, write a new positive one. These will help you celebrate the good patterns your family has brought to you.

You might want to write down the members of your immediate family—parents, siblings, and grandparents. (If you have nontraditional family experiences, use those individuals you consider to be significant mentors.) Think about how you related to each of these family members and what you learned about yourself from them. How did they treat you? What were some ways they hurt you? What were some ways they made you feel valuable and special? Remember that the negative responses may come easier than the positive ones. Be patient and allow the positive ones to percolate to the surface of your memory.

Write at least three examples of both negative and positive statements that you remember your family member saying to you. Feel free to write down more as they come to you. You will use them later in the Moving Forward section of this chapter.

Present Relationships

As you review past relationships, take some time to examine your current relationships. Many times our present relationships are a direct reflection of the quality and content of our past relationships. If our childhood experience is negative, we often choose to engage in similar relationships as adults. For example, a child with alcoholic parents will often be drawn to an alcoholic spouse. A child growing up with an overbearing parent will often choose to marry the same sort of person. We seek the familiar, even if that familiar is negative.

Write down the significant people in your life not included in the previous list of family, listing each person by name and relationship. Special people in your life need not be confined to family. They can be coworkers, friends, mentors, acquaintances. How does each person relate to you? Is it a positive or a negative way? Does the present relationship mirror a past relationship? Look back over the list of activities you created in chapter 4, and be aware of any people who are represented under major activities in your life. For example, you may not think of a coworker as a significant person in your life until you realize how much time you actually spend together. Look for that positive, filling person who might emerge out of a draining activity. This is definitely a significant person in your life!

What does each relationship tell you about yourself? Who are you in that relationship? As you examine your role in each, consider whether you are a *filler* or a *drainer* in that relationship. If you consider yourself to be both, is the positive or the negative more predominant? Do you believe that person would concur with your assessment?

It is an unfortunate fact of human nature that we often emulate the very patterns we dislike. If you have several draining relationships, you will want to examine your own role to see if you are the common negative denominator.

Virtual Void

Ironically, the very thing we turn to for increased connectivity with others is proving to be the biggest disconnection point in our lives. Not only are we distracting ourselves from face-to-face interactions, but the virtual relationships we're prioritizing are often lacking in the most important connection point of all—the intimacy of in-person warmth and sincerity.

To detect the presence or extent of your virtual void, ask yourself:

- What am I doing online?
- How am I connecting with others?
- What is the content of that connection?
- Would I be willing for my spouse or members of my family to view all of my online activities and content?

- Relationships are formed through time—what relationships do I have online?
- What emotional needs are being met through these online relationships?
- How would I feel if I were unable to connect online for a day? a week? a month?
- How many nonfamily online relationships do I maintain?
- Of those relationships, how many do I keep strictly online, meaning I don't talk or visit but only connect online?
- Are there any online relationships or activities that pose a threat or provide competition to my in-person relationships?
- Am I willing, within the next week, to modify, limit, or sever any online relationship or activity that poses such a threat?
- If so, what is my step-by-step action plan for doing that?
- If I'm not willing, what is holding me back? Be specific. Am I willing to seek professional help to overcome this barrier?

As difficult as it may be to face your answers to these questions, do not underestimate the power of these truths to naturally lend themselves to your transformation. Simply observing and accepting your behavior as it exists now will naturally inspire you to make more informed (i.e., healthier) decisions in the future.

Moving Forward

Depression can come when we feel bound to repeat the negative patterns of our past. Through an honest evaluation of our past and present relationships, we come to understand who we are and what we bring to each of our relationships. While it is important to acknowledge the past and understand its effects on the present, it is also important to know that you have the opportunity to make positive changes for your future.

Look over your journal, and if you haven't done so already, identify two positive relationships. These are people you will want to intentionally spend time with. If you have not approached them yet, consider discussing with them your desire to recover from depression and enlist their support and aid in your recovery. Be open with them about your feelings. Commit to strengthen your relationship, and articulate your desire to mutually support each other.

As you recover from depression, you may find that your circle of support will not come from the members of your family. It may be necessary for you to use other relationships to provide the support you need. Your family may be too close to objectively view your recovery. Members of your family may not be prepared to accept the truth you've uncovered through this process. Don't allow their lack of acceptance to deter you in seeking the truth. The goal is not to protect the family; the goal is to recapture a life filled with optimism, hope, and joy. If you need to discard flawed family patterns and perceptions, it is your prerogative as an adult to do so.

If this is the case, the time will come when you should be able to include your family in your recovery. They may need some additional time to process the same information and come to their own understanding. You can give them time without apologizing for your recovery. Those who love you will come to accept the positive changes in your life, even if you present yourself differently. This change, away from depression and toward recovery, will benefit not only you but also your current relationships.

In the next chapter, we will look at positive, proactive steps you can take to strengthen key relationships, mend fractured relationships, and modify negative relationships. In your battle over depression, these relationships act as supply lines. Damaged relationships weaken your ability to stay in the fight. Positive relationships nourish your spirit and bolster your ability to overcome.

Use Your Journal to Review Chapter 5

- Moving Forward Phrase: *I will pursue positive relationships that nourish my spirit and help me overcome my depression.*
- The journal work in this chapter is centered around understanding and tracking your past and present relationships. Use these statements to help direct your thinking about your family growing up:

  > The good things my family taught me about
  >   life are...
  > The negative things my family taught me about
  >   life are...
  > The good things my family taught me about
  >   myself are...
  > The negative things my family taught me about
  >   myself are...

- Write down those with whom you are currently in relationship with, as well as those in your past who were influential but who may no longer be an active part of your life.
- Evaluate whether these relationships are or were filling or draining. Be honest about any responsibility you may have in their being draining.

6

Rebuilding Relationships

Family cannot be blamed for depression.
Family may be a factor, but you are
responsible for your own recovery.

"Your sister's on the phone!" Callie's husband yelled over the noise of the kids and the television. Callie's sister was not his favorite person.

"I'll take it in the bedroom," she responded, seeking a small island of quiet in the sea of chaos at her house. "Watch the broiler for me, and make sure the garlic bread doesn't burn, okay?" His eager nod meant he was relieved to be handling dinner and not her sister.

"Hi, Kay. Sorry about that. It's dinnertime here, and it's a little crazy." As usual, her sister was oblivious to anything other than her latest agenda.

"I called to talk to you about getting together at Thanksgiving this year. I've got the whole thing planned, and I need to be sure your flight doesn't mess up everything." Callie stifled her laugh so Kay wouldn't hear it. When Kay said "mess up," it sounded just like when they were kids, and Kay was accusing her of "messing up" their room. Callie was the younger of the two and as such had always been considered the root of every problem in Kay's teenage life.

Arguing was pointless, so Callie listened as Kay outlined the schedule of events. Waiting for Kay to pause for breath, she took one of her own and staked out her position. "Kay, I appreciate everything you've done to plan this for Mom and Dad. Bill and I will try to get tickets that don't interfere, but we've got to stick to our budget this year, so if we can get a cheaper flight at a different time, we'll do it. Hopefully, the rest of the family will understand since we're flying such a long way." Looking at her husband standing quietly in the bedroom doorway, Callie saw Bill smile, potholder in hand, the thumb of the quilted mitt solidly in the air.

When Pain Is Gain

Dealing with problems isn't pleasant, but sometimes problems can be beneficial. This is especially true if a problem in one area of your life leads you to uncover and deal with a problem in another area. The first problem could be considered a blessing, in that it helps you to become aware of the second.

As we discussed in the last chapter, dysfunction in relationships can contribute to depression. Overcoming depression can give you the motivation you need to move beyond the status quo in your life. Those who have moved beyond depression speak of a renewed understanding of what is truly important and vital in their lives. While none of them rejoiced over their depression, they have been able to articulate how their walk through depression made them a stronger person, a more compassionate friend, or a truly grateful family member.

Realizing the ties your family may have to your depression can be very painful. It means accepting a reality about your upbringing you may have been avoiding. It means reliving a pain you may have found overwhelming. It means giving up your childhood desires for the sake of who you are now as an adult. This is transition, and significant transition at that. Understanding the benefits that await you on the side of recovery makes this transition easier. As you redefine your family relationships, the insight and understanding you gain will assist you in strengthening all of your relationships—from your family of origin to your current family, from good friends to casual acquaintances, from business contacts to coworkers.

Take a Good Look

Up to now, you have been focusing on others. Before you continue examining others, pause for a moment and take a good, deep look at *you*. Perhaps the most fundamental relationship you have is not with someone else—it is with yourself. Though you interact with others, you are also in constant communication with yourself through self-talk. This inner dialogue sets the stage for how you respond to life.

When you are depressed, your self-talk can become one sided, centered on a negative dialogue of despair, regrets, frustration, confusion, and doubts. The voice of forgiveness is rarely heard, and the chorus of optimism, hope, and joy are drowned out.

Take some time to think about how you treat yourself. Are you your own drainer or filler? Do you make it a habit of pointing out the positive? Is your self-talk a constant stream of emphasizing the negative? How do you talk to yourself when you make a mistake? How do you talk to yourself when negative circumstances occur? Imagine you've just had an automobile accident. No one is injured, but your car is badly damaged. The accident is your fault. Write down three things you would say to yourself.

You might write down negative comments about yourself, your driving habits, your worth as a person, your intellectual capacity. Or possibly, you will write comments that will only partially accept responsibility for the accident. In other words, you may have a tendency to magnify your blame or minimize your responsibility. Neither of these perspectives is helpful to the situation.

Magnifying is harmful because it crushes you as an individual and leaves no room for forgiveness. Minimizing is harmful because it does not allow you to learn from the situation and become a better person. Neither option allows you to experience the truth and then grow.

Take the example of this hypothetical situation, and consider that you carry on conversations like this with yourself multiple times each day. It's usually not over something as dramatic as an automobile accident, but the cumulative effect can be significant. It's the internal dialogue you have with yourself as you're driving to work, as you carry out tasks during the day, as you interact with others, and as you react to hundreds of small events.

If your self-talk is out of balance, either magnifying or minimizing your role in each of the day's events, your ability to maintain a healthy relationship with yourself is compromised. When you magnify, you make yourself a victim to your own perfectionism. When you minimize, you keep yourself a captive to your own mistakes.

One way you can work toward a healthier relationship with yourself is through more realistic and truthful self-talk. For example, in the situation of the automobile accident, it is healthy to acknowledge your role in the accident. It is also healthy to realize that accidents do happen. It is healthy to be grateful that no one was injured and that you have insurance to help repair the damages. So, as you are talking to yourself about the accident, you neither beat yourself up nor let yourself off the hook. (For a wonderful book on the process of healthier self-talk, please consider *Self-Coaching: The Powerful Program to Beat Anxiety and Depression* by Joseph J. Luciani, PhD. This book goes through a program for modifying your self-talk, regardless of your personality type, with lots of helpful activities. It helps you evaluate your pattern of self-talk and find ways to make it more truthful and positive.)

There is great value in acknowledging and affirming the truth, both about situations and about yourself in those situations. Having the courage to accept and integrate the truth builds self-esteem. In the scenario of the automobile accident, it is true that you were at fault for the accident, but it is also true that you accept responsibility, that you pledge to do all you can to make it right, and that you put the accident into context and allow it to make you a better driver. You can feel good knowing that you have done the right thing, even in a difficult situation.

Often, other people will not tell you the truth, either because they don't know the truth or they are threatened by it. In any case, it may be that the only person who will tell the truth is *you*. That is why it is imperative that your self-talk affirms the truth when no one else around you will. That is why the first step to overcoming depression is to *recognize,* promote, and sustain optimism, hope, and joy. Life-affirming self-talk allows you to recognize the truth.

Know Your Friends

In today's social media–saturated world, no analysis of relationships would be complete without proper attention to the criteria you set for your friends—online and off. If you are engaged in online relationships that you consider to be prominent sources of support and companionship—lending them as much weight as you would any offline friendship—do yourself a favor and be sure to hold the relationships up to the same standards you should expect of anyone you call a real friend.

As mentioned earlier, I have an entire book devoted to the topic of media, technology, and social networking. Below is the list of descriptors I give in *#Hooked* for determining the strength of friendships, online and off:

- *Trust:* Friends trust each other because each has proven to be trustworthy. When tempted to betray the friendship in some way, they have held fast to the needs and feelings of the other person instead.

- *Honesty:* One of the hallmarks of true friendship is living within an atmosphere of truth. This truth, however, is not a harsh, brutal presentation but one done in love, compassion, and tenderness. To a friend the truth is not a weapon; it is a balm. There is safety in the honest words of a friend, even when those words hurt.

- *Understanding:* True friends understand each other. They know the background and context of each other's lives. They know the *what* of things, but they also know the *why* of things. Friends know which way the other will jump and how far.

- *Acceptance:* Friends understand the precarious position they put themselves in by being a friend. Proximity sometimes equates to pain where human beings are concerned; friends acknowledge this pain as an acceptable consequence of the friendship.
- *Mutual benefit:* True friends add to each other's lives. Often the benefit isn't always equal, but it is mutual. True friends monitor the relationship to ensure there is both give and take, refusing to allow it to become chronically one sided and draining.
- *Sacrifice:* There are times when friendship calls for sacrifice. It can be a sacrifice of time, money, energy, resources—a reordering of priorities to put the needs of friendship first.
- *Affection:* At the heart of all friendships should be genuine affection one for the other. Friends enjoy each other; they like to be together because of the way they feel about each other.

This is not to say you should discount any online relationship that does not live up to these standards. It is simply a means of helping you keep such relationships in perspective. You could very well develop a genuine friendship with someone you meet online, and you may already have. But the chances of this happening with multitudes of people is unlikely, and if you feel otherwise, a more rigorous assessment of these friendships is probably in order.

Changing Relationships

Using your journal, look again at your relationships. You will be going over and examining each one through a variety of filters. In the earlier chapters, you were asked to identify drainers and fillers. You gained insight into how these relationships affect you and your ability to move beyond depression.

Consider which relationships need to be mended, which need to be modified, and which need to be strengthened. If you have relationships that are both draining and filling, it may be possible to make changes in a relationship, mending it, so that the filling aspects of the relationship will begin to outweigh the draining. If you have relationships that are and will continue to be draining relationships, you will need to look at ways to reduce the amount of negativity and damage they cause you. Relationships that are filling are the ones you will want to strengthen. Whether you mend, modify, or strengthen, it is important to realize that you have the ability to affect and change relationships. Remember, the most important relationship you may come to change is the one you have with yourself.

Mend

Your patterns and perceptions have molded your personality, and these personality traits will invariably enter into relationships you have. While you are aware of how others affect a relationship, you also want to be aware of where you are setting the parameters for relationships.

Most adult relationships are two way. A changed relationship, though, does not require both parties to change. A change can occur if only one person in the relationship commits to change. Before you approach the other person, you can examine your own role in the relationship and make positive changes. In changing yourself, you change the dynamics of the relationship.

As you consider which relationships you need to mend, consider how the other person sets the tone for the relationship. Examine realistically your role in any fraying of that relationship. Remember that you need to honestly evaluate the relationship, neither magnifying nor minimizing your contribution to its strengths and weaknesses. If the relationship is fractured, think back to a time prior to the splitting away. What happened? Have the two of you ever spoken about what happened? Are you aware of how the other person views the relationship? How have you interacted with this person since the relationship became frayed?

Think back to how you speak to yourself. As you realize the tone of conversation you are having with yourself, you should become more aware of the conversations you are having with others. Often, our conversations with others are reflections of the conversations we have with ourselves. If you identified a significant relationship where you are the drainer, consider the type and content of conversations and interactions you have with that person.

To assist you in honestly assessing this relationship, ask yourself the following questions:

- Do you expect this person to protect you emotionally?
- Do you expect this person to hurt you emotionally?
- Do you allow this person to manipulate you?
- Does a part of you feel safer whenever this person is in control?
- Does a part of you only feel safe when you, and not this person, are in control?
- Are you manipulating this person through your depression?
- Do you have a habit of discounting or minimizing your own needs to this person?
- Do you prevent this person from knowing and filling your needs?
- Do you derive your sense of self-worth from your ability to meet this person's needs?
- Do you actively promote yourself as a martyr in this relationship?
- Do you avoid solving problems in this relationship?
- Are you unable to relax and have fun in this relationship?
- Are you afraid to be truthful in this relationship?

If you have answered yes to any of these questions, this indicates an out-of-balance relationship and one you will want to mend or modify.

There is much that you can do to mend any relationship. Most people are willing to change themselves when they witness and experience genuine change in the other person. By taking the first step toward mending the relationship, you can assist the other person in taking his or her own steps toward healing, until you are brought together and the relationship is mended.

(Drs. Les and Leslie Parrott have written a very helpful book titled *Relationships: An Open and Honest Guide to Making Bad Relationships Better and Good Relationships Great.*)

Modify

What do you do with relationships that you have tried to mend but remain broken? Once you honestly assess the relationship and realize you are neither magnifying nor minimizing your responsibility in the brokenness of that relationship, you may need to accept the reality that changes are necessary.

Sometimes we are in relationships with extremely negative people. They are our primary drainers. Sadly, these individuals are often members of our family, who through family ties feel they have a right to act as an emotional, physical, or financial drain on our lives. If you continue in these same kinds of draining relationships, your ability to overcome depression can be seriously compromised. When a draining relationship brings you to a continued state of depression, it is time to change that relationship for your own health and well-being.

This can be a significant decision, not to be taken lightly. To help you determine if a relationship is one you need to modify, consider whether or not this person is at the source of, or contributes to, your negative patterns, perceptions, and deceptive self-talk. If this is the case, you will want to modify your relationship with this person, and possibly even eliminate it altogether.

If this person is a member of your family, it may not be possible for you to cut off contact. Wherever possible, you should attempt to mend this relationship, hopeful of change by the other person. If you have tried, making the changes you feel you are able to make, yet it still remains a significant drain on your optimism, hope, and joy, then you will need to modify the boundaries of that relationship.

What this means is that you will need to interact with that person less. You may need to assert yourself more. You will need to decide under what conditions you are able to continue with this relationship and then communicate these boundaries to that person. It will be up to the other person to decide whether or not to continue in relationship with you under those conditions. If this person refuses to accept your boundaries and wishes to continue with the destructive status quo, you withdraw from the relationship until the other person modifies behaviors toward you and respects the boundaries you have set.

Communicating these boundaries should not be done in a confrontational manner. Boundaries should be stated in a natural, matter-of-fact way. When Callie was speaking to Kay, she listened to what her sister had to say and then simply stated her boundary about the family visit. She didn't fight with her or argue with her. She didn't cut her off or raise her voice. Instead, she stated her boundary along with a reasonable explanation for the boundary. You do not need to apologize for or feel guilty about setting such a boundary. Boundaries are normal and healthy for all relationships. (For an insightful and helpful discussion of the role of boundaries, see *Boundaries* by Drs. Henry Cloud and John Townsend. There are several books on boundaries in different relationships in this long-running series.)

Generally, when you are mending a relationship, you are setting boundaries for your own behavior. When you are looking to modify a relationship, you are setting boundaries for the behavior of others.

Strengthen

As you look over your list of significant relationships, there may be one or two "diamonds in the rough." These may include a positive relationship that you want to spend time and energy strengthening. The way to strengthen these relationships is to make the best contribution to the relationship that you can. Healthy relationships have the capacity to grow even stronger as both people work to enhance the connection. Consider using the following skills to strengthen relationships:

- Approach the person with an attitude of gratefulness. Few people appreciate being taken for granted. If this person is a significant filler in your life, let her know that. Express your gratitude for the relationship.

- Speak the truth to this person, whether you are talking about that person or about yourself. Trust between two people is enhanced when truth is spoken.

- As you talk with this person, allow for differences of opinion. People enjoy being able to talk about themselves and how they feel. This will give you the opportunity to really learn about this person.

- Release this person to make decisions for himself in the relationship. Don't give in to a need to control or relinquish decisions. Healthy relationships are two way. Don't burden the other person with your need to either take control yourself or force him to make all the decisions. Work together and allow for differences.

- Be respectful of the boundaries she feels are necessary for the relationship. If you want her to respect your boundaries, you must respect hers.

- Ask forgiveness when you make a mistake. Don't try to hide it. And don't try to magnify or minimize it—be truthful.

- Be accountable to that person. This grants permission to that person to comment on your actions. Being accountable is a mark of a committed friendship.

- When you do have a conflict with this person (and you will), be motivated to resolve the problem instead of trying to be "right." Remember to focus on the strength of the friendship and not on the problem.

- Exercise forgiveness, for that person and for yourself.

Moving Forward

Many people have things in their past that they are ashamed of. Guilt becomes a chain around their optimism, hope, and joy. In order to be free, you need to forgive yourself.

Write in your journal three things you still harbor guilt over. Write down any patterns of self-talk you use when you think about your guilt over these things. Now go to a mirror and look yourself square in the face. Say to yourself out loud, "I forgive myself for _____." Say this pardon at least three times for each of the things you have written down. Say this pardon over and over until you integrate this forgiveness. Consider these things gone so you needn't mention them again in your self-talk. You have forgiven yourself. Give yourself permission to move beyond them. Remember, you are accepting the truth of what you have done, and you are embracing the greater truth of the joy of forgiveness.

Now that you have experienced this joy, you can choose to give it as a gift to someone else. Consider a relationship on your list that needs your forgiveness to begin the mending process. When you are confident of your ability to forgive, make contact with that person and tell him or her the good news.

There are few things more beautiful or vital in relationships than forgiveness. We are flawed people and, as such, will cause hurt and be hurt. Forgiveness is the balm that allows these hurts to heal. Forgiveness is not blind to the truth nor a blank check to pain. When there is a wrong, there is a debt. Forgiveness is when you have a clear view of the truth and choose to release others from their debt to you.

As you move forward in your recovery from depression, don't forget the role of forgiveness. If you are thinking of the forgiveness you need, move beyond the guilt and condemnation. As you consider the forgiveness you need to extend to others, release the blame, anger, and resentment. You control who and what you forgive.

Each of us needs to determine the boundaries of our forgiveness. In order to recognize, promote, and sustain optimism, hope, and joy, those boundaries should be as large as we can possibly make them. Within those boundaries, we will be able to experience many satisfying relationships.

Take steps to mend existing relationships, modify damaging relationships, and strengthen affirming relationships. You will then be well positioned to create new ones, which is a wonderful hope for the future.

Use Your Journal to Review Chapter 6

- Moving Forward Phrase: *I am the person with the most positive effect on all my relationships.*
- Your journal work in this chapter is based upon an understanding of your relationships and making concrete decisions about which relationships you need to mend, which you need to modify, and which you need to strengthen.
- Write a narrative about each of your significant relationships. Note when they began and what impact each has had on your life. Be sure to write *Mend, Modify, or Strengthen* next to each.
- For each Mend relationship, write down three steps you can take to mend that relationship, including changing your own actions.
- For each Modify relationship, write down three steps you can take to impose healthy boundaries, along with how you plan to communicate those boundaries.
- For each Strengthen relationship, commit to making contact with that person this week and express your appreciation for the relationship.

7

Physical Causes of Depression

Few people realize the impact their physical state has on their ability to overcome depression. Depression is not a mental condition but a debilitating whole-body condition that must be addressed physically as well as mentally.

Angela sat in her car, bewildered by the prescription she'd just gotten from her doctor. *I can't believe it's come to this,* she thought. *I don't want to take it, but I don't want to keep on going this way either. I just want me back. I just want to feel good again.*

She had a hard time remembering the last time she felt good. It started with the death of her mother two years before and had just kept spiraling downhill from there. She felt tired, unmotivated, overwhelmed. She was losing the ability to concentrate, to focus. She couldn't remember the last time she had a good night's rest. The doctor had given her sleeping pills after her mother's death, and now she used them regularly, but the sleep felt drugged, not natural or refreshing.

Nothing felt natural or refreshing anymore. She should be over her mother's death by now, but she still didn't feel right. That's why she'd gone back to her doctor. And she had another prescription from him, this time for an antidepressant. Angela agreed she was depressed, but she couldn't imagine how taking a pill was going to make her feel good again.

But she was willing to do it because she wanted the old Angela back: the Angela who used to laugh, the Angela who enjoyed her job, the Angela who found time to be with others. Over the past two years, her world had shrunk along with her joy and self-confidence. About the only things that hadn't shrunk were her hips. For that alone she was willing to try the pill. She had to do something—she couldn't go on like this.

The Rise in Prescription Antidepressants

While there is no dispute that the incidence of depression is growing, the response to this growth is changing. The trend has been away from traditional psychotherapy and toward a pharmaceutical solution. As reported by *Scientific American,* "Between 1996 and 2005 the percentage of psychiatry office visits involving psychotherapy decreased from about 44.4 percent—already a significant decline from the 1980s—to 28.9 percent. One of the main causes for this 35 percent reduction in psychotherapy, the study's authors say, is the increasing availability of psychiatric medications with few adverse effects."[7] In short, more people are being diagnosed with depression, more of them are being given medication, and fewer are receiving counseling. The whole-person approach is being replaced by the promise of a "magic pill."

Accompanying the increase in prescription medication is a lack of acknowledgment by the medical community of the role that physical health and nutrition play in addressing depression. The focal point of depression treatment is not what the body can do for itself but rather how the body, specifically the brain, is viewed as defective. Because the emphasis of study is on a neurological chemical imbalance, it isn't difficult to understand why the preferred solution is chemical, or pharmaceutical, in nature.

Today's emphasis on medications centers around a new classification of drugs called SSRIs (selective serotonin reuptake inhibitors), which includes Prozac, Zoloft, and Paxil. Serotonin is one of the body's important neurotransmitters, which assist in brain functions including mood, sleep, mental alertness, and sexual responsiveness. These drugs certainly have a place in relieving symptoms of severe depression, but an overemphasis on these drugs does not incorporate alternative approaches helpful for alleviating depression.

Dr. Peter R. Breggin, in 1994 sounded the warning regarding this emphasis on psychiatric drugs to treat depression in his groundbreaking book *Toxic Psychiatry*.[8] In his book, he looked into the not-so-distant future and the possible consequences of this treatment trend, predicting, "Innumerable adults with solvable personal problems will end up taking drugs, getting shock treatment, or being locked up in mental hospitals—or all three."[9] Dr. Breggin's subtitle for this book speaks loudly to his preferred method for helping those with depression: *Why Therapy, Empathy, and Love Must Replace the Drugs, Electroshock, and Biochemical Theories of the "New Psychiatry."*

Concerned about this trend toward drugs alone and away from other types of therapy, Dr. Breggin followed up *Toxic Psychiatry* with *Talking Back to Prozac*.[10] This book discusses specific information related to Prozac, a top-selling antidepressant, and Dr. Breggin's concerns about harmful side effects. He frames the problem this way: "Increasingly, life is becoming a contest between pills—exemplified by Prozac—and life itself. People are giving up on life in favor of pills. They are abandoning the struggle to embrace life for the ease of swallowing a pill. There is an enormous cost attached to this choice."[11]

Sigmund Freud, perhaps prophetically, said, "We use talk now until we understand the chemistry." The above-mentioned statistic reported in *Scientific American* illustrates the prescription perception that with the introduction of more and more antidepressant medications, talking (counseling or psychotherapy) is no longer as important. This sets up a scenario where medication alone is touted as the definitive cure for depression. Sadly, this is not the case.

Of course, none of this is to discount the pivotal role pharmaceuticals can and should play in treating extreme forms of depression. For instance, the National Institute of Mental Health conducted a study of the drug ketamine on those with bipolar disorder. In findings published in *Biological Psychiatry,* it's been revealed that a single dose of ketamine has dramatic antidepressant effects within forty minutes of taking it. And it is also the first and only drug that not only "significantly reduced suicidal thoughts" in those with bipolar depression but it did so within one hour of dosage.[12]

What New Brain Science Tells Us About Depression

The more we learn about depression from a scientific approach, the more encouraging the possibilities for innovative treatments.

The latest in brain science shows that people with a history of depression have a smaller hippocampus than those who have no such history. As explained by WebMD, this is notable because

> A smaller hippocampus has fewer serotonin receptors. Serotonin is a calming brain chemical known as a neurotransmitter that allows communication between nerves in the brain and the body. It's also thought that the neurotransmitter norepinephrine may be involved in depression.[13]

It remains to be seen why the hippocampus is smaller and what purpose this knowledge could serve in depression treatment. However, any scientific understanding of depression can, at the very least, provide some level of comfort to those for whom their depression seems to have no source.

In fact, developing a medical understanding of depression is often one of the keys to successful treatment. The more people understand about how depression is tied to brain activity beyond a person's control, the less shame and guilt they may feel about their thoughts, feelings, and behaviors, and the more likely they are to respect and follow through with treatment. This is one of many benefits Dr. Daniel Amen notes about SPECT scans (single-photon emission computed tomography). In his SPECT-imaging research, Dr. Amen has been able to identify seven types of anxiety and depression:

1. pure anxiety
2. pure depression
3. mixed anxiety and depression
4. overfocused anxiety and depression
5. temporal-lobe anxiety and depression
6. cyclic anxiety and depression
7. "lights are low" anxiety and depression

This is not to suggest that all brain images indicating these types of depression look the same as the next. On the contrary, depression looks as different in each individual brain as it feels in each individual person.

Specifically, these SPECT images are able to identify three areas of activity in the brain: areas that are working well, areas of low activity, and areas of high activity. It's based on these images that doctors can more accurately prescribe treatment. For instance, if the SPECT scan reveals low activity, the last thing needed is a prescription antidepressant that lowers brain activity. Yet that is precisely what happens in countless cases, meaning people are being needlessly treated with medications that are only compounding the problem.[14]

Whole-Person Help

In a whole-person approach, the entire body is recognized as an important component in depression. The whole-person approach accepts the body as a complex organism and looks for systemic reasons for depression. This approach is supported by Dr. Robert A. Anderson, a past president of the American Holistic Medical Association. In the *Clinician's Guide to Holistic Medicine,* Dr. Anderson makes the recommendation that a definitive diagnosis of depression should not be made until physical conditions have been surveyed.[15]

The body is not merely along for the mind's ride into depression. The body is an active participant with the capacity to aggravate or improve symptoms of depression. The whole-person approach looks closely at the physical, emotional, environmental, and spiritual factors involved in depression. Understanding the complete picture of an individual's depression leads to effective whole-person solutions. For many people, their first stop on the road to recovery from depression is into a physician's office. After all, they *feel* bad. Whatever the factors leading to their depression, many will attempt to obtain a medical diagnosis for physical symptoms:

- changes in sleep pattern, either sleeping too much or too little
- changes in appetite, losing appetite, or feeling like they can never get enough
- changes in weight, correlating to the change in appetite, resulting in either putting on excessive weight or losing weight
- fatigue and a lack of vitality
- trouble remembering or concentrating
- heightened anxiety or irritability
- a failure to thrive

These are all physical signs that point to depression and can arise from a variety of physical causes.

Although this chapter will include extensive information about physical causes, the intent is not to make you feel overwhelmed by the number of factors that could be present in your depression. Rather, they are presented to enlighten you to the very real possibility that what is going on inside you includes a physical component and is affecting your resolve to overcome depression.

After you have made a mental decision to intentionally recognize, promote, and sustain optimism, hope, and joy, your body may not be in a position to follow your mind. Your body may be holding you back. In order to go forward, you need to examine what is happening to you physically and make changes to assist in your recovery.

Addressing physical conditions can have a dramatic effect in overcoming depression. As stated by the Mayo Clinic, "Physical health conditions can sometimes cause or worsen depression. Examples include thyroid disorders, chronic pain, anemia and heart problems."[16]

In the whole-person approach, the body itself is considered to hold its own special key to the reason behind depression. Physical illnesses are explored as well as physical conditions that may not be diagnosed or readily apparent. Even when blood work and medical examinations are done, the physical culprits involved in depression can be overlooked.

Like a detective, you need to be informed and persistent to discover the truth. As you continue in the journey to reach beyond your own depression, be aware of any physical factors impacting your ability to sustain recovery.

Hot on the Trail

Evaluate the following possibilities. You may immediately recognize some as being present in your life. To diagnose others, you may need to obtain the professional expertise of a medical doctor, who understands the role of physical conditions in depression. You may need a nutritionist trained in the physiological ramifications of depression. Where possible, look for an orthomolecular psychiatrist. This is a medical doctor with a specialty in psychiatry, who investigates the link between environmental factors and mental conditions.

The U.S. National Library of Medicine National Institutes of Health says of orthomolecular psychiatry, "The functioning of the brain is affected by the molecular concentrations of many substances that are normally present in the brain. The optimum concentrations of these substances for a person may differ greatly from the concentrations provided by his normal diet and genetic machinery. Biochemical and genetic arguments support the idea that orthomolecular therapy, the provision for the individual person of the optimum concentrations of important normal constituents of the brain, may be the preferred treatment for many mentally ill patients."[17]

It is important for you to remember that each of these physiological conditions can be successfully addressed by and factored into the whole-person approach. As you read over the following factors, consider whether or not they could have an impact on your own depression, and use your journal for tracking. On a single page write three headings: "Definite" – "Probable" – "Possible." Under "Definite," put factors that you know are involved in your depression. Under "Probable," write factors you highly suspect have an impact on your depression or your ability to recover. Under "Possible," place factors you think might be involved but need further exploration.

This list can be useful when you feel it necessary to seek the advice of a health-care professional, as it can provide a starting point for an in-depth investigation into your depression's physical factors.

To begin we will examine several known causes of depression. We have seen them demonstrated in the lives of countless clients. Many times, individuals came in suffering from depression without really understanding why. Other times, clients who initially came to us because of an addiction or eating disorder sought help for depression as well. The list of possible contributors is long, but take this time to read through this chapter and note any that seem relevant to your life as you are reading.

Hypoglycemia

Helen came to the Center suffering from anxiety and depression. Her moods swung from hopelessness and lethargy to being stressed out and anxious. If it wasn't one, it was the other. Both were taking their toll, and she wanted an end to them. Helen was tired of never feeling settled. She had become terrified she was bipolar because of her roller-coaster moods. It was this fear that finally propelled her into counseling. In addition to her therapy, Helen set up an appointment to see our nutritionist. What was mysterious to her was obvious to him. Helen had hypoglycemia, which was a major source of her depression and anxiety.

Over the course of her adult life, Helen developed a pattern of hypoglycemia based upon her eating habits and food choices. She preferred quick, calorie-rich foods, eaten sporadically, with large amounts of caffeine throughout the day. Because she worked for a newspaper, Helen's duties were stressful and time sensitive. Many times she put off eating, subsisting instead on high-caffeine beverages and sweets, consumed on the run. The caffeine and sweets propelled her headlong into nervousness and anxiety as her blood sugar levels spiked. The resulting crash of insulin to counter this massive sugar dump in her system brought feelings of depression and physical depletion. At these low times, Helen doubted her abilities, fretted over her age, and raged over any mistake. When Helen hit rock bottom, she questioned whether she was really capable of doing her high-stress, high-profile job. Her body was playing right into her fears of unworthiness and inadequacy to handle her job.

Hypoglycemia is more commonly known as low blood sugar or the "sugar blues." The body's main source of fuel is glucose, which is a form of sugar. Glucose is produced by the body through the consumption of carbohydrates, sugars, and starches. Glucose is absorbed into the bloodstream during digestion. Glucose that is not needed is stored in the liver as glycogen. When the amount of sugar in the blood is insufficient to fuel the body's activities, hypoglycemia occurs. While this condition has not been universally accepted as a cause of depression, even skeptics will agree that hypoglycemia can cause weakness, mental dullness, confusion, and fatigue. All of these symptoms, when taken together, can exacerbate depression.

Some in the medical community, especially those schooled in holistic medicine, do make the connection between depression and hypoglycemia, including the U.S. National Library of Medicine National Institutes of Health.[18]

Food and caffeine became Helen's drugs of choice. Food, so abundant in this country, is often used as a form of self-medication and comfort, especially high-sugar, high-fat foods. These foods flood the bloodstream with an energy surge. While using food to treat feelings of depression may prove temporarily effective, the resulting crash of low blood sugar can make you feel even worse. As you look at your own cycles of depression, look for a connection between what you eat and how you feel.

Here are common signs of hypoglycemia:

- headache
- nervousness
- confusion or disorientation
- hunger
- weakness
- rapid heart beat
- slurred speech
- tingling lips
- sweating

(For further information on hypoglycemia, please see the following titles from the Resource List at the end of the book: *Sugar Blues* by William Duffy; *Potatoes Not Prozac: Are You Sugar Sensitive?* by Kathleen DesMaisons, PhD; and *Get the Sugar Out* by Ann Louise Gittleman, MS, CNS. You can also visit our website at www.aplaceofhope.com and take our Hypoglycemia Quiz.)

Other Physiological Conditions

Heart disease—A recent study has shown that one out of every five people who suffers a heart attack will become depressed. It is understandable how such a traumatic event in one's life could contribute to a state of depression. Conversely, a link between depression and heart disease was found in a study at the Johns Hopkins School of Hygiene and Public Health, which reported that 1) those with heart disease were more likely to be depressed than healthy people, and 2) depressed people who had heart attacks were four times more likely to die within the next six months as people who were not depressed.[19]

What is not known is why. Speculations include a weakened immune system due to the stress hormones secreted during bouts of depression. Depressed people may be neglecting themselves or not taking their medications properly. Whichever the case, you will want to note whether or not you, or a family member, has a history of heart disease. Often the reduction of blood flow and circulation that occurs with heart disease can cause a loss of physical vitality, which you may be interpreting as depression.

(For more information on heart disease and diet, look into *The Carbohydrate Addict's Healthy Heart Program: Break Your Carbo-Insulin Connection to Heart Disease* by Dr. Richard F. Heller, Dr. Rachael F. Heller, and Dr. Frederic J. Vagnini.)

Anemia—This condition is also known as iron-poor blood. Symptoms of anemia, similar to depression, include fatigue, weakness, and lethargy. It is difficult to experience mental alertness, optimism, or energy when your body is physically run down. If you are a woman experiencing depression, be aware that women have a much higher incidence of anemia. This could be a cause in your general lack of vitality.

Apnea—Sleep apnea is a condition where the air passages in the throat close off during sleep. It is more common in those who are overweight and older, as the muscles in the throat lose rigidity and become limp upon relaxation. The throat basically closes in on itself, depriving the body of oxygen. The body will fight back by causing the person to gasp to reopen the air passages. Those who suffer from sleep apnea fluctuate between gasping and suffocating. This pattern severely strains the body and makes getting a good night's sleep impossible. The resulting symptoms are fatigue, mental confusion, and lethargy—all associated with a state of depression. Though this is a serious condition, it can be treated successfully through surgical and nonsurgical methods.

Celiac Disease—This is a condition in which the immune system attacks the food protein gluten. In the process, the small intestine is damaged, making it difficult, if not impossible, for the body to absorb zinc, tryptophan, B vitamins, and other essential nutrients. The absence of these nutrients affects the body's ability to produce serotonin, the deficiency of which is known to be linked to depression. For this reason, those with celiac disease should follow a gluten-free diet. A blood test can help identify celiac disease, and an endoscopy of the intestinal lining can confirm it.[20]

Diabetes—This is the body's inability to regulate its own blood sugar. This condition is treated with insulin through ingestion (pill), absorption (patch), or injection (shot). While insulin delivery systems continue to be refined to mimic the body's own natural levels, they are still far from perfect. The constant up-and-down stress of elevated versus low blood sugar levels can compromise the body's ability to regulate important nutrient absorption and hormonal levels, which provide protection from depressive mood swings. It should be noted that prolonged periods of hypoglycemia can lead to adult-onset diabetes.

Seasonal Affective Disorder (SAD)—This is also known as "the winter blues." This depressive cycle is tied to the body's pattern of melatonin secretion. Melatonin is a hormone that regulates the body's biological clock and coordinates the sleep-wake cycle, including temperature control. Melatonin is produced in the dark and is in greatest production during winter months. However, due to winter's shorter days, melatonin may be produced either earlier or later in the day, thus throwing the body's cycle off track. That's why those who suffer from SAD may experience moderate to intense periods of depression during the winter. As you observe patterns to your depression, be aware of the time of day and the season of the year. Those who suffer from SAD will find that their depression is definitely linked to a lack of sunlight and the long, dark days of winter.

Heredity—Simply put, depression appears to run in families. While no definitive study pinpoints a depression gene, there is research that suggests a family link. Half of manic-depressives have at least one parent with the disorder, and a study of twins showed that identical twins were twice as likely to share depression as fraternal twins. You need to educate yourself on your family-health background, a worthwhile endeavor in any case. Be aware especially of parents or siblings who have experienced depression. Remember that their depression may be undiagnosed. Talk to relatives if immediate family members are no longer alive.

Dehydration—Most people don't drink enough water. When the body is dehydrated, one of its main detoxification methods is compromised. If toxic substances are not flushed out of the system, they remain in the body and lead to a toxic buildup. In addition, water is the body's main lubricant for its important processes. A lack of water impairs the body's ability to perform vital functions. Dehydration can cause fatigue, weakness, dizziness, and mental dullness. Caffeinated and alcoholic beverages promote dehydration. Those who use these types of drinks to feel better can actually aggravate their dehydration and heighten the symptoms that mimic depression.

Reactional Hyperphagia—It's no secret we tend to crave comfort foods when we're stressed. This doesn't bode well for people whose stress stems from their inability to lose weight, particularly if they're experiencing reactional hyperphagia. In this condition, emotional stress affects brain chemistry and hormones in such a way that the body craves "fullness," even if there is no physical basis for it.[21]

Endocrine Disorders—Research shows that most patients with hypothyroidism, a thyroid deficiency, have symptoms consistent with clinical depression.[22] When the endocrine system, comprised of the thyroid and adrenal glands, is not working properly, through either over- or underfunctioning, depression has been a result. However, doctors rarely check the thyroid, so its connection to evident depression often goes undiagnosed. Symptoms of hypothyroidism include

- anxiety and nightmares
- difficulty losing weight
- dry skin
- easy weight gain
- impaired concentration and memory
- menstrual irregularities
- mood swings
- severe fatigue
- thinning eyebrows
- thinning hair
- yellow skin from poor conversion of beta carotene to vitamin A

If you have any or all of these symptoms, ask your doctor to check your thyroid; a simple blood test can help determine whether it is functioning properly or not.[23]

Impaired Homocysteine Conversion—Homocysteine is a nonprotein amino acid, the presence of which in the body must necessarily be converted into the amino acid cysteine. This conversion requires adequate amounts of folate, B12, B6, and zinc in the body. So it is deficiencies of these nutrients that impair the homocysteine-to-cysteine conversion, resulting in homocysteine buildup in the body, the overabundance of which has been linked to depression.[24]

Hormonal Fluctuations

Puberty—The onset of puberty in both girls and boys can result in depression. Boys may experience decreased depression. Girls may experience increased depression as puberty progresses. Pubertal depression can be due to physiological, hormonal, and cultural changes experienced during early adolescence. Simply put, puberty is a time of difficult transition, both physically and emotionally. The combination of societal and physical factors is potent and can be overwhelming to young people fighting to emerge from childhood into adulthood.

Postpartum Depression—This is also known as "the baby blues." Many new mothers experience mild depression after the birth of a child. Symptoms usually fade within a week. While the cause has not been definitely linked, a drop of estrogen and progesterone levels five days after delivery may bring on feelings of depression. In a very small number of women, postpartum psychosis can result, with severe depression and hallucinations. Studies indicate that if you have a history of depression prior to pregnancy, you are at a higher risk for developing postpartum depression.

Premenstrual Syndrome—This syndrome is increasingly linked to the depressive symptoms of despondent mood, irritability, exhaustion, and bouts of crying. Research is being done on the link between depression in PMS and lowered levels of melatonin and serotonin. Because of the link between PMS and depression, if you are a woman, you will want to be aware of how your monthly cycle coincides with your feelings of depression.

Menopausal Phases—During menopause in women, the body produces less estrogen, progesterone, and testosterone, all vital hormones. Progesterone and testosterone production can decrease at a faster rate than estrogen, upsetting the proper balance and causing estrogen dominance. With this imbalance, mood changes can occur and depression may result. These hormonal fluctuations can also affect the operation of the thyroid gland, causing hypothyroidism, discussed above.

(For more information, check out these books: *What Your Doctor May Not Tell You About Premenopause: Balance Your Hormones and Your Life from Thirty to Fifty* by John R. Lee, MD, Jesse Hanley, MD, and Virginia Hopkins; and *What Your Doctor May Not Tell You About*

Menopause: The Breakthrough Book on Natural Progesterone by John R. Lee, MD, and Virginia Hopkins.)

Low Testosterone—During the natural aging process in men, testosterone production is decreased. Higher testosterone levels are known to produce vitality, lean muscle mass, lower body fat, and enhanced sexual performance. The lowering or loss of these traits can produce depression in men as they age. This impacts the physical as well as psychological changes in men. Studies show a significant link between low testosterone and depression in older men.[25]

(For more information on testosterone, please see the reference in the Resource List for *The Testosterone Syndrome: The Critical Factor of Energy, Health, and Sexuality—Reversing the Male Menopause* by Eugene Shippen, MD, and William Fryer.)

Allergies and Sensitivities

Karla felt terrible. She'd gone to her doctor feeling run down and listless, but blood tests proved inconclusive. Unable to pinpoint anything physical, her doctor suggested she try counseling to overcome her deepening feelings of despair. Karla knew something was wrong, but she couldn't find any relief. She didn't understand how counseling would help—after all, she felt bad. How could just talking about it help? Karla would soon be amazed.

Through counseling, Karla understood that she had developed a short list of "safe" foods. Over the years, Karla had traded variety for a set number of foods she decided were safe for her to eat.

Karla grew up with a mother who resented being "chained to the kitchen." She paid little attention to the food she was feeding her family. It was poorly planned at best and contaminated at worst. Karla learned which foods her mother prepared were safe, and which ones could be bad and were to be avoided. This pattern continued through adulthood.

On the list of Karla's safe foods were breads and rolls because it was easy for her to tell if they were stale. If the bread was blue and hairy it was bad. Generally breads were safe. Bread made her feel good, and she ate plenty of it.

This overconsumption produced an allergic reaction to wheat when she was an adult. The reaction produced cravings for wheat, which Karla was only too happy to indulge. On and on the cycle went. As a result, Karla's immune system was completely stressed out. She developed fibromyalgia—or muscle pain—and migraines. The more she craved, the more she ate. The more she ate, the greater she hurt. Her despair grew, and her hope of finding relief faded.

Through psychotherapy, Karla was able to understand her emotional connection to food and to add more variety to her "safe" list. Through nutritional therapy, Karla was able to break the cycle of cravings, and she started to feel better. Her pain decreased, her headaches lessened, and her optimism began to return.

As in Karla's case, a food allergy or sensitivity can arise from an over-consumption of certain foods. The most common food allergies we see are to wheat and dairy products. Why? Because wheat and dairy products are such a large part of today's diet. As they are eaten over and over, day in and day out, the body can build up an intolerance to them, resulting in sensitivity or an allergic reaction to the product.

The irony is that the body responds to food allergies and sensitivities in the opposite way one would expect. Instead of naturally rejecting these products, the body craves them. Similar to a drug fix, when you ingest the product your body is allergic or sensitive to, it produces a momentary relief in symptoms. However, after that initial relief, symptoms return even stronger, producing a greater craving. Such is the vicious cycle of food allergies and sensitivities.

As you consider whether or not you have a food allergy, you will want to be aware of what you are eating. Do you eat a variety of foods? Do you experience intense cravings for a certain type of food? Again, we see the greatest number of food allergies to wheat and dairy products, as well as chocolate and refined sugar. Do you experience gastrointestinal distress after eating certain foods? In the past several years, more and more people have experienced allergic reactions to common foods, such as peanuts and bananas.

Be aware not only of what you eat but how you digest what you eat. In your journal, track for three days what you are eating, how much, and the intensity of your desire for that specific food, as well as any digestive difficulties, including gas, bloating, diarrhea, or constipation.

Food allergies can actually be reactions to food additives, as opposed to the food itself. Much of the food we eat is exposed to pesticides and chemical substances, which are used to increase yield, decrease spoilage, and enhance shelf life. These substances can also lead to food allergies and sensitivities. What you see is no longer always what you get when purchasing food and produce today.

Allergic reactions stress your central nervous system through an ever-alert immune system. When the body recognizes a substance as an allergen, the immune system is deployed to deal with the "foreign" invader. It is constantly on guard, using physical resources. One of the symptoms of a food allergy or sensitivity can be depression, due to this depletion. If there are other physical factors contributing to depression, food allergies and sensitivities are just one more straw pressing on the proverbial camel's back. Research has revealed this link between depression and allergies.[26]

Please keep in mind that allergies and sensitivities can be to other factors besides food. There are people who are allergic or sensitive to molds and mildews in their homes or workspaces. Over time, these allergies depress the immune system and can contribute to the body's inability to repair itself, function at optimum levels, and regulate imbalances. Again, a stressed-out immune system is an immune system constantly on guard, at the ready. The price for this vigilance is fatigue and loss of vitality, which can complicate a state of depression.

The good news is that when an allergy is discovered and alleviated, often the feelings of depression lift. Psychiatrist Dr. Abram Hoffer puts it this way: "When one is relieved, so is the other. Treatment of the allergy will then, in most cases, cure the depression. I've seen this in several hundred patients over the past years and I can no longer doubt this conclusion."[27]

As you are investigating whether or not you've developed an allergy or sensitivity that could be contributing to your depression, consider these allergic symptoms:

- a history of common allergies, such as hay fever, asthma, or eczema
- sinusitis
- dark circles under the eyes, also known as "allergic shiners"
- weight fluctuation due to water retention
- eyesight difficulties
- fatigue
- mental fogginess
- irritability
- high sensitivity to noise, light, or temperature

Allergies and sensitivities can flare up during times of emotional distress or trauma, in the presence of alcohol or drugs, and when yeast infections are present.

Yeasts

At the Center, we are especially aware of the effects of yeast, specifically *Candida albicans,* on the body. Almost 75 percent of our eating-disorder clients have experienced recurrent yeast infections. As we treat them for these yeast infections, their physical energy improves, their insatiable cravings decrease, and their depressive symptoms are remarkably lightened.

You will know whether or not you have an overgrowth of yeast in your system, having gone to the doctor or pharmacist time and time again due to bladder or vaginal yeast infections. Or you might not be aware of yeast as an issue.

Count your yes answers to the following questions, taken from *The Yeast Connection* by Dr. William Crook:[28]

- Have you taken repeated or prolonged courses of antibiotics?
- Have you been bothered by recurrent vaginal, prostate, or urinary infections?
- Do you feel "sick all over," yet the cause hasn't been found?
- Are you bothered by hormone disturbances, including PMS, menstrual irregularities, sexual dysfunction, sugar craving, low body temperature, or fatigue?
- Are you unusually sensitive to tobacco smoke, perfumes, colognes, and other chemical odors?
- Are you bothered by memory or concentration problems?
- Do you sometimes feel "spaced out"?
- Have you taken prolonged courses of prednisone or other steroids, or have you taken "the pill" for more than three years?
- Do some foods disagree with you or trigger symptoms?
- Do you suffer with constipation, diarrhea, bloating, or abdominal pain?

According to Dr. Crook, the scoring is as follows:

For women, if your score is nine or more, your health problems are probably yeast connected.

For men, if your score is seven or more, your health problems are probably yeast connected. If your score is ten, your health problems are almost certainly yeast connected.

Yeast infections are a common problem among women, as eight to ten times more women will experience them than men. Most yeast infections are vaginal, but bladder infections can also be a sign of a yeast overgrowth. Yeast is a fungus (like mold, mildew, or mushrooms) that lives in the digestive tract, the vagina, and just about anywhere in the body that is warm and moist. We have even seen clients who had such an overabundance of yeast in their system that it was growing in the folds of their skin. Yeast can also be found in the sinus tract, ears, and mouth. An overgrowth of yeast in the mouth is commonly known as thrush.

Some yeast is normally found in the digestive tract, where it lives in balance with healthy digestive bacteria. However, there are situations where the population of healthy bacteria is diminished, allowing the yeast, especially *Candida albicans,* to overproduce. Yeast feeds on sugar, so the more yeast in your system, the more your body will crave sugar. As the yeast feeds on sugar, it produces toxins as by-products.

One of these toxins is ethanol, a known central nervous system depressant. These toxins are dumped into your system where the body must work overtime to flush them out. Overgrowth of yeast in the small intestine interferes with protein digestion and amino-acid absorption. In addition, the toxicity of the yeast can cause the body to become allergic to foods it tolerated before.

Overproduction of yeast can occur if we inadvertently suppress the amount of healthy bacteria in our digestive tract. This suppression can be done as an unintended consequence of treating other physical problems. Antibiotics in use today are called broad spectrum, meaning they kill a wide variety of organisms. The downside to these medications is the destruction they cause to our healthy digestive bacteria. *Candida albicans,* however, is not affected by antibiotics. Friendly bacteria can be decimated by antibiotics, while yeast is left to thrive and grow, unrestrained, in your intestinal tract.

Yeasts can do further damage. They weaken the lining of the intestinal wall, so food substances can actually "leak" into the bloodstream before being fully digested. These underdigested food particles are then interpreted by the body as foreign invaders, triggering an immune reaction. This is a condition known as leaky gut syndrome. As the body works overtime to fight off this leakage, fatigue and a general loss of vitality result.

Yeast overgrowth can be a factor in chronic fatigue syndrome. This is a condition where fatigue is not relieved by sleeping. The person never feels rested or refreshed. With the immune system under constant assault, vital resources and nutrients are being diverted, unavailable for the body's general use to restore and repair itself. As a result, the person continually feels run down. In such a condition, depression can often take hold.

Multiple Chemical Sensitivity

Nancy got to where she couldn't stand to leave her house. Anytime she went out, she would return sick to her stomach, complaining of a headache or nausea, and spend anywhere from the next hour to several days in bed. Her family, worried she was experiencing agoraphobia, convinced her to go into counseling. It was a major undertaking for them to bring her in to the Center. It wasn't long before we discovered that Nancy did not suffer from agoraphobia but rather multiple chemical sensitivity. Her family thought that Nancy got sick because she couldn't stand to be away from her house. In truth, Nancy got sick because of what she came into contact with when she did leave her house. In short, Nancy wasn't afraid of the outside world; she was allergic to it.

There are certain people who have a heightened sensitivity to the chemicals that permeate our lives. Perfumes, deodorants, cleaning products, solvents—the list goes on and on. Our culture is awash in chemicals, and some people have an extremely low tolerance level. For those individuals, a woman's perfume at church can produce a migraine headache. A man's cigar in a crowd can lead to nausea. The cleaning solution used on the floor in the grocery store can lead to muscle pain.

Too often, these suffering individuals are considered hypochondriacs by those around them. In pain, confused about the source, fearful that it might just be all in their heads, these individuals can plummet into depression. This is especially true when they have been unable, for whatever reason, to find relief. Recognizing the source of their physical reactions is like opening a curtain in a darkened room. Understanding allows the person to make choices about what they expose themselves to, empowering them to be in control of their environment instead of the other way around. With nutritional support, their weakened immune systems can be rejuvenated, mitigating some of their more extreme allergic reactions.

Environmental Factors

Lead

Lead is a natural by-product of our industrialized society. As a heavy metal, lead is toxic to the body in large doses. Toxic levels can accumulate in our bodies over time through small amounts stored in the body's fat cells. A depressed mental state can occur from lead poisoning. Following are situations to be aware of when evaluating your exposure to environmental lead:

Food in cans—Lead-soldered cans have a rougher seam than non-lead-soldered cans, which have a smooth seam or a rounded bottom. Food stored in lead-soldered cans have significantly higher levels of lead. The level of lead in these foods can soar when the can is opened and exposed to air, and when the food inside is not removed but stored in the can itself.

Eating ware—Underfired pottery can contain large amounts of lead, especially if imported from other countries with different environmental standards. Lead crystal is also something to be aware of. Even when the material of the pottery is lead free, there are lead-based enamels that can flake off or emit lead fumes. Again, be aware of pottery from outside the United States and produced nonprofessionally.

Older plumbing fixtures—Lead was often used in older plumbing and piping. Water that stands in those pipes will absorb lead and contaminate your household drinking water.

Paint—From the 1950s and earlier, paint was routinely made with lead. Even if that older contaminated paint has been covered over, any sanding or scraping can create lead-filled dust, from which lead can be inhaled or absorbed through the skin.

Asian medications—Certain medications prepared by traditional Asian methods can contain toxic levels of lead.[29]

Aluminum

Aluminum can cause depressive symptoms and is found in the following:

Antacids—Many have aluminum in them, as well as lead, found in bone meal and oyster-shell calcium supplements.

Dialysis—Bones in those who undergo chronic dialysis have aluminum levels of nine to fifty times the norm.[30]

Aluminum cookware—These pots and pans can leach aluminum into acidic liquids, including fluoridated water.

Tap water—In some cities with outdated water-treatment facilities, tap water can contain excessive aluminum.

Aluminum salts—These ingredients can appear in foods, processed cheese, spices, and baking powder.

Personal care products—Some antiperspirants and deodorants rely on a form of aluminum.

Old appliances—Corroded air conditioners or aluminum-core water heaters can give off aluminum.

Mercury

Mercury poisoning can produce depression, and this highly toxic heavy metal can be found in the following:

Mercury amalgam dental fillings—When present in our mouths, they continue to emit mercury with every bite, every chew, when we grind our teeth, or when we drink hot liquids.

Over-the-counter pharmaceuticals containing thimerosal or sodium ethyl mercury—These mercury-based ingredients can be found in certain antiseptics, ointments, cosmetics, laxatives, eyedrops, contraceptive gels, and douches.

Broken equipment, such as fluorescent lighting, thermometers, and certain scientific equipment—As the use of fluorescent lighting increases due to its energy efficiency, the mercury in old tubes presents an increasingly difficult disposal problem.

Household products—This category includes items such as fabric softeners, floor polishes, wood preservatives, adhesives, fungicides, paints, dyes, tattoos, and fabrics.

Fish products—Some seafood absorbs and stores high concentrations of mercury found in their environment. People who eat this seafood will build up high levels of mercury. This has been known to occur in tuna, swordfish, shellfish, and seaweed.

Occupational exposure—Professionals who routinely work with mercury, such as dentists and dental personnel, embalmers, photographers, painters, and those working around batteries or pressure gauges can have elevated levels of mercury in their bodies.

Copper

An overload of this otherwise important nutrient can occur from water, especially soft water standing in copper plumbing or water treated with copper sulfate by water districts. Cigarettes are a source of copper, as are copper cookware and certain fungicides containing copper sulphate.

Organic Solvents

These are found everywhere, and the most troubling are those that are petrochemical based. They are found in everything from the pen you write with to the whiteout you use to correct a mistake. They are in perfumes and glues, motor oil and cleaning products. According to *Dealing with Depression Naturally* by Syd Baumel, "At the Centers for Disease Control and elsewhere, researchers have repeatedly found an abnormal degree of depression, irritability, mental impairment, and other symptoms of 'painters syndrome' in persons chronically exposed to acceptable occupations levels of VOS [volatile organic solvents]."[31] Those with increased sensitivity to these organic solvents are at greatest risk for depressive symptoms due to exposure.

Self-Administered Substances

Alcohol—This mood-altering drug is a known depressant and is toxic to the body in large doses. In addition, as discussed before, alcohol promotes dehydration.

Tobacco—This is also a known depressant. The resulting sedative-like effect is why cigarettes are a major drug of choice for many people.

Birth-control pills—These pills impair the body's conversion of nutrients into serotonin, which enhances mood and sleep. As such, birth-control pills have been known to contribute to depression.

Antihistamines—These over-the-counter allergy medications can cause fatigue, lethargy, and mental dullness, mirroring feelings of depression.

Caffeine—Many people use caffeine as a stimulant. However, if you ingest over five hundred milligrams of caffeine per day, the opposite effect can occur. Too much caffeine acts as a depressant, causing fatigue. This is especially true when caffeine is combined with tobacco.

Antibiotics—As mentioned before, these bacteria-killing medications are often indiscriminate. When they kill healthy bacteria, especially in our digestive tracts, our bodies are susceptible to unhealthy bacteria and yeasts. An overabundance of unhealthy bacteria in our digestive tracts inhibits our ability to absorb essential B-vitamins and important digestion-assisting enzymes. With the decreased ability to absorb and assimilate nutrients, symptoms of depression can occur.

Medications

In addition to all of the factors you've just read, there are currently over two hundred medications on the market that have been shown to have the potential to cause depression. These include certain blood pressure medications, drugs used to treat Parkinson's disease, diet pills, arthritis medications, ulcer medications, and seizure medications. Even medications used primarily as tranquilizers, such as Valium and Halcion, have been shown to cause depression under certain conditions.[32] In the fine print, under "Side Effects," depression is listed as a possible consequence.

Moving Forward

Realizing the number of physical elements that can be contributing to your depression is probably overwhelming. But the operative word here is *can*. Not all of these factors will be present in your depression. This information is provided so you will realize how vital your body is to your recovery. Your body is a remarkable, complex system with an amazing ability to heal. It is also a finely tuned instrument that can be stressed out of balance by factors listed in this chapter. Your body can act as your adversary, thwarting your best intentions to make changes, or it can act as your ally, supporting those same intentions.

In the next chapter, we will look at positive steps you can take to address physical factors in your depression. But first, it is important for you to take a good look at your own body. Evaluate what you are putting into your body and onto your body, and what conditions surround your body. You are on a search to remove any physical contributors to your depression.

Depending upon your circumstances and what you discover, you may want to seek professional assistance. There are medical personnel trained to investigate and evaluate these physical components to depression. For some people, it will be imperative that they seek out medical and nutritional help in overcoming their depression, especially if they have heightened sensitivities and allergies, or have been exposed to environmental toxicities.

Your journal work for this chapter is as a depression detective. You should already be tracking how and what you eat. In addition, take a tour of where you live and evaluate your surroundings. What substances are parts of your day? Include personal-care products and household-cleaning products. Check under sinks and in laundry areas. Look in medicine cabinets and on your bathroom counter. Track all of the chemicals in your home. These are the chemicals you expose yourself to on a regular basis. Be sure to include soaps, cleaners, aerosols, and sprays. Remember to track what is in use by other people in your home. Just because you are not using these products does not mean you are not exposed to them.

Now think about your usage of these products. Can you pinpoint any that seem to give you a headache or to which you can remember a physical reaction? What about smells? Do any cause your stomach to be queasy? These are products you will want to put first on your list to replace or avoid. Remember that these can be products you use or those in use by others in your home.

Next, be aware not only of what is in your house but also your house itself. Do you have carpets? Allergists will tell you that carpets are one of the first things to get rid of if you are experiencing heightened allergies at home. Carpets are repositories of all kinds of bacteria, mold, mildew, allergens, and pests. They have been known to contain irritating chemical substances such as adhesives and formaldehyde.

As you are considering your home, try this experiment. The next time you enter your home after a long absence, go into each room and smell for any prevalent odors. Search for chemically based odors or those that cause a physical reaction. You may be able to identify an area in your home where fumes are seeping in and causing you to experience a physical reaction. Ask yourself how often each room in your house receives fresh air. Are certain parts of your home closed off?

Use this same evaluation on your work environment. For some, your workspace will be as important as your home. Be especially cognizant of industrial pollutants or substances you may be exposed to at work, by touch or smell. Ask questions about cleaning products used. Often industrial cleaners in work situations come with a much higher concentration of chemicals than the household variety.

Remember, you will want to evaluate your other home—your body—the home you take with you wherever you go. It cannot be emphasized enough that what you eat can either help or hinder your recovery from depression. Your food and fluid choices can be some of your most powerful friends or foes in the struggle over depression.

Over the next three days, keep track of everything you eat and drink. Note the time you ate or drank, what it was, the quantity, and how you were feeling at the time. Also make a note if you have a change in mood during the day. Please be honest as you track your eating and drinking patterns. It will not benefit you to "cheat" on this tracking. Rather, being honest will help you determine if there is a pattern developing to your depression, especially as it relates to hypoglycemia or food allergies and sensitivities. Please be aware that often your body will crave the very substance it is allergic to.

You are searching for causes; the effect is already known—your depression. If there are physical problems occurring through how and where you live your life, you need to know what they are so you can develop a strategy for overcoming them. This strategy is possible.

There are many things that can adversely affect the body's ability to combat depression, and there are specific ways to bolster your body's depression-fighting systems. The next chapter will help you take what you discover in your search and put it to use, crafting a personalized strategy for dealing with physical causes of your depression.

There are ways. There is hope. Start looking now.

Use Your Journal to Review Chapter 7

- Write down what you eat and drink for three days. Note how you are feeling as you eat and as you digest your food. Be aware of any gas, bloating, diarrhea, or constipation.

- Take a tour of your house and note the personal-care products and chemicals in use by yourself or others in your home. Be aware of any strong reactions when exposed to any of them.
- Scout out your workplace for the presence of harmful chemicals or products. Especially be aware of any substances you come in contact with on a regular basis due to your job.
- Moving Forward Phrase: *It is important to my recovery to care for my body.*

8

Replenishing the Body

> While the number of potential factors in physical depression is large, the good news is a small number of positive changes can bring about enormous benefit.

"Perfection!" Sally held up the warm, plump globe, deepening red. Gently, she disengaged the fruit from its stem and set it down in her basket next to the squash, beans, and lettuce she'd already harvested. Even her tomatoes were doing well this year! It was a bigger garden than she'd ever attempted, but her labor was certainly bearing fruit.

The next-door neighbor chided her in a good-natured way about puttering around so much, but she didn't let it bother her. Taking care of her garden was like taking care of herself. She'd put off doing both for far too long. Frankly, she'd let her garden and her life get choked out by too many weeds.

Little by little over the years, Sally had traded in the important for the urgent. As her career as a nurse gained steam, it began to roll over the other activities of her life. After all, her work was important, and Sally was very good at it. The better she got, the more pressure she took on. The more pressure she took on, the less she began to enjoy life. In a life-giving profession, she had less and less to give. After years of providing help, Sally decided one day it was time to ask for some. It wasn't selfish; it was necessary.

The idea to replant her neglected garden came while she was talking with her counselor, who asked a question about what she enjoyed doing. It took her a moment to answer because, in her current life, she had trouble thinking of any. She had things she did, important things, but not necessarily things she enjoyed. That's when she spoke of the gardens she'd helped with when she was growing up.

"What was it about gardening you liked so much?"

"Caring for something," Sally had finally answered. "Watching over it and taking care of it. Knowing I could help something to grow. I hadn't really thought of it before, but that's the same reason I went into nursing."

"Have you ever thought of yourself that way?" her counselor asked. "As someone to be cared for? What are you doing to help yourself grow?"

From the seed planted that day, Sally set out to care for her garden and for herself.

Taking Care of Yourself

Our bodies are truly remarkable, complex and resilient yet adversely affected by simple and subtle conditions. In the last chapter, you took steps to identify physical factors involved in your depression. Since you are unique, you will have a different set of circumstances. You may be able to pinpoint quickly areas you want to investigate, or you may have difficulty defining one cause or another. Possibly, you are bewildered by the numerous factors that could be affecting your body and contributing to your depression.

Again, the causes are many, but the solutions are few. Over the years, we have been able to identify five lifestyle choices you can make that will dramatically improve your health and your optimism and that will bolster your emotional resiliency. They are not complicated, and they are based on age-old common sense. They are healthy eating, good nutrition, proper hydration, physical motion, and restful sleep. You should integrate each of these five lifestyle choices individually and collectively as ways to fortify your body against the ravages of depression.

Eating Healthy

In a society where food is everywhere, this would appear to be a simple task. Yet it is not. Much of the food available today is produced for convenience, not nutrition. Additives are injected to increase shelf life, nutrients are removed by manufacturing processes, and sugars and salts are added to please the palate. These foods are called "devitalized."[33] They hold the promise of health and nutrition but are unable to deliver. They include

- processed foods
- white flour
- refined sugar
- white rice
- "junk" foods

In our fast-paced world, these foods are attractive because they are convenient and quick. When your energy is depleted through depression, the siren song of these foods can sound even louder. You must resist their lure and intentionally make other choices. Think of "devitalized" foods as fragmented foods—they contain only a portion of what is promised. The essential nutrients have been stripped away, and only the fragments remain, along with a host of unhealthful additives, preservatives, pumped-up sugars, fats, and salts. (This is also the working definition of most "junk" foods.)

Instead of fragmented foods, look for whole foods. These include

- fresh fruits and vegetables
- whole grains
- low-fat dairy products (eggs, milk, butter, cream, cheese)

- legumes (beans)
- lean meat
- nuts
- oils (especially flaxseed, olive, and canola oils)
- poultry

How do you use these two lists to enhance your health in eating? Here's how the whole foods instead of fragmented foods might exchange for a typical breakfast. Instead of fragmented foods such as high-sugar, heavily processed breakfast cereal, try a whole-grain cereal, either hot or cold. Instead of using sugar if the cereal is cold, cut up a banana and put it on top. If the cereal is hot, crush up the banana and mix it in. Because it takes your body longer to digest whole foods, you will be able to maintain a more balanced sugar-insulin ratio and stay "full" longer. The fiber in the cereal and the banana will also help your entire digestive and elimination system.

A fragmented lunch could be a stop at a fast-food restaurant for a burger, fries, and shake. These are highly processed foods, so much so that often a fast-food shake doesn't actually contain any dairy products at all. A whole-food lunch, on the other hand, could be a turkey sandwich on whole-wheat or multigrain bread, with fresh lettuce, tomatoes, onions, peppers, or cucumbers. Instead of fries, try grapes or baby carrots, even whole-grain chips. Instead of a shake, choose herbal tea, milk, or water.

A whole-food dinner could be fresh squash, mushrooms, and onions sautéed in olive oil and served with marinated meat or poultry and whole-grain pasta. Dessert could be fresh berry compote.

Fragmented snacks are everywhere, from salty chips to empty-caloried sweets, from candy to heavily salted meats and jerkies. Go into any convenience store, and you will find them front and center. Whole-food snacks would be any cut-up fruit or vegetable. A whole-grain roll or muffin. A fruit-and-grain bar. A mix of seeds, nuts, and dried fruit.

Eating healthy does not mean forgoing a stop at a fast-food restaurant. At most fast-food restaurants, it is possible to find healthier alternatives to the typical "meal deal." Many have a grilled-chicken alternative, and any restaurant can be directed to cut down on the amount of fatty condiments used on what you order. You can also choose fast-food restaurants with ethnic or sandwich-style meals. Often, your choices of healthy eating are enhanced when you get away from burgers and fries and choose restaurants that allow you to dictate what goes onto your food. As the dietary choices of more people become healthier, the restaurant industry will follow. You can accelerate that decision by intentionally selecting where and what you eat.

Eating healthy is not only what and where you eat but also how you eat, so keep the following in mind as you make whole food choices:

- Don't eat too much. Stop eating before you actually feel full. Intentionally start out with smaller portions, and wait a few minutes before deciding if you need more.
- Eat a variety of whole foods. Healthy eating is not limited eating; rather it is intentional eating that encompasses a medley of choice. Remember, produce is more than just apples and lettuce. Many times our choices are dictated by what we are used to and what we grew up with. Be adventurous and try different whole foods. In this way, you will have a greater opportunity to obtain necessary nutrients from what you eat.
- Choose a healthy ratio of food. Eat more fruits and vegetables than breads. Eat more breads than dairy products. Eat more dairy products than meat and poultry. Eat more meat and poultry than sugars and fats. This is the *food pyramid* of recommended dietary choices. There are diagrams of food pyramids in grocery stores across America. Ask your produce manager for one. For healthy eating tips, visit www.choose myplate.gov.

- Choose your fats intentionally. Healthy eating doesn't eliminate fat from the diet; rather it chooses the types of fats consumed. Avoid fats comprised of trans-fatty acids and saturated fats. Choose instead the fats found in moderate amounts of real butter, cheese, and polyunsaturated oils, such as flaxseed, olive, and canola.

Depressive thinking is tied to reactive thinking. Eating patterns can also be reactive. Stress eating is a perfect example, which women are especially at risk for, as revealed in a study published in the *American Journal of Clinical Nutrition*. Women burnt out at work were much more prone to emotional, "uncontrolled" eating than women who experienced no such work burnout.[34]

Just as recognizing, promoting, and sustaining optimism, hope, and joy are intentional choices, so is eating healthy. One supports the other. It is empowering to know that you can choose everything you put in your mouth. In overcoming depression, you want to make each bite count.

(For more information about healthy eating, please see the following books by the author: *21 Days to Eating Better* and *Losing Weight Permanently: Secrets of the 2% Who Succeed*.)

Supporting Your Body Nutritionally

Eating healthy is a wonderful beginning, but overcoming depression will require the additional nutritional step of supplementation.

There are four categories of supplements important to good health in general and in overcoming depression specifically. They are vitamins, minerals, amino acids, and essential fatty acids. Deficiencies in these substances have been clinically shown to produce symptoms of depression.

Not Pill Pushing

When Candice first came to see me, she was concerned about her health. As we talked, I asked her about her eating habits and what, if any, supplements she was taking. Candice told me she took so many supplements, she couldn't remember which ones or how many.

On her next visit, she showed up with two-handled shopping bags full of the supplements she took. There were hundreds of bottles. Candice didn't so much eat as swallow. Overdosed with so many nutritional supplements, her body didn't know when or what to actually eat. Whatever the latest "fad" supplement, Candice had it. But she never stopped taking any of the others when she added a new one. Candice's health was a supplement nightmare.

When I pointed out the danger to Candice, she seemed shocked and surprised. Because we incorporate nutritional supplements and products into our whole-person approach, she thought I would praise her for her two shopping bags, not warn her. Gently, I explained that we advocate nutritional support, not supplement overload.

As you incorporate nutritional supplements into your recovery from depression, it is important that you understand what you need to take and why. The nutritional supplements that we find the most useful for the broadest range of clients are given below. However, your search may require that you obtain the services of a nutritionist, naturopathic physician, or an orthomolecular psychiatrist. At the very least, ask questions of someone knowledgeable whenever you purchase a nutritional supplement. If you don't know what it does or why it's important for you to take, wait until you can find someone who can assist you.

From our experience, here is what we generally recommend for clients:

A high-potency, readily assimilated multivitamin. The one we sell at the Center is called Multi-Mineral Plus and comes with or without iron. When choosing a good multivitamin, you will want to look for high bioavailability; in other words, a formula that your body can easily absorb. It doesn't do you any good to take a vitamin and mineral supplement that washes out of your system, unused, every time you go to the bathroom.

Make sure any multivitamin you choose includes the following vitamins and minerals:

- Vitamin B1 (thiamine)—This vitamin aids our brains in converting glucose to energy. Unconverted glucose becomes fat, so you want to be able to use the food you eat for energy. You'll feel better and lose weight. Oftentimes, clients who have boosted their B1 intake find that it is easier to cut out excess sugars and still have energy.

- Vitamin B3 (niacin)—This essential vitamin has been shown to be effective not only for treatment of depression but also for lowering cholesterol.

- Vitamin B6 (pyridoxine)—Low levels of this vitamin have been found in clinically depressed patients. It has been effective, therefore, in treating depression, as well as PMS and vitamin B6 deficiency due to prolonged use of birth-control pills. Vitamin B6 has been shown to aid in serotonin production, through enhancing conversion of an important amino acid, tryptophan, into serotonin.

- Folic Acid (folate, folacin)—The critical nature of this vitamin has been underscored recently by the government recommendation that it be given to all women of childbearing age. Folic acid has proven antidepressant effects. Research has shown that the lower the level of folic acid, the longer and more severe the depressive episode.[35] Those with low folic acid levels not only were found to experience greater depression, but they were also found to be less responsive to pharmaceutical antidepressants.[36]

- Vitamin B12 (cobalamin, cyanocobalamin, hydroxocobalamin)—This essential vitamin can prove tricky because it doesn't digest fast enough in many supplements to stay in the body. For those with a vitamin B12 deficiency, it can be delivered via a nasal gel, under-the-tongue drops, or injection.

- Vitamin C (ascorbic acid)—This essential vitamin has proven to safeguard the body from disease, colds, stress, and depression. In one study, a single megadose of vitamin C outperformed the placebo in eleven manic and twelve depressed patients, cutting depressive episodes 40 percent to four hours.
- Choline—This is considered a nonessential nutrient because it is normally produced by the human body. If your choline level is low, however, depression can result. Conversely, large doses of choline can worsen depression.
- Magnesium—This mineral is an essential nutrient found to be helpful in lowering total cholesterol and supporting production of good cholesterol.
- Calcium—Necessary for healthy bones, this mineral is often used in conjunction with magnesium. (At the Center, we use a product called Cal 2: Mag 1 when additional supplementation of these two minerals is indicated.)
- DHEA—This is the most abundant hormone in the human body, so it stands to reason that any deficiency would make a significant physical impact. Studies show that those with depression symptoms often have low levels of DHEA. Supporting this is evidence that DHEA supplementation helps ease depression symptoms. In a study conducted by the National Institute of Mental Health, participants who had previously been diagnosed with depression were given DHEA supplements. After just six weeks, half of the participants experienced a 50-percent decline in depression symptoms.[37]

While most people are aware of the role of vitamins and minerals in nutritional supplementation, some may not be as aware of the role of amino acids. As stated on LiveStrong.com, "The body requires 22 essential amino acids to build the proteins that fight infection, regulate growth and influence mental state. While most of these amino acids are synthesized by the body, there are several that must come from the food we eat and the supplements we take. According to Intelegen.com, many people do not get enough tryptophan, an essential amino acid that leads to serotonin production. Serotonin is vital for regulating mood and appetite. A deficiency of serotonin can lead to depression and anxiety as well as to a tendency to eat more high-carbohydrate foods."[38]

Our clients use a product called Amino Gram Forte. Amino-acid supplements can include phenylalanine, tyrosine, and taurine. Phenylalanine and tyrosine are closely related and are used by the body to produce neurotransmitters, including norepinephrine, which regulates the ability to experience pleasure. A lack of this neurotransmitter is thought to be a significant factor in depression. Taurine is produced by the body for the most part, although small amounts can be obtained from food. Increasing availability of taurine has been found to have an antidepressant effect.

In addition to Amino Gram Forte, we also recommend our clients use a product called 5HTP, which stands for 5-hydroxytryptophan. This substance is converted in the body into serotonin. By augmenting your 5HTP levels, the body is given a boost in serotonin production.

Fat has developed a rather sinister reputation of late, but fat is an essential component of life. For nutritional support, it is important that you obtain the right amounts of the right fatty acids. Look for fatty acid supplements with GLA (gamma-linolenic acid), ALA (alpha-linolenic acid) and EPA (eicosapentaenoic acid). Correct metabolism of these fatty acids are vitamin and mineral dependent, so they should be taken in conjunction with a good multivitamin and mineral formula.

Additionally, there is excellent data on the efficacy of herbal support for mood and diminished depressive symptoms. According to the Mayo Clinic, scientific evidence supports the effectiveness of St.-John's-wort (*Hypericum perforatum*) for mild-to-moderate major depression.[39] Another herbal supplement, ginkgo biloba, has also been touted as an antidepressant, but while it does improve brain functioning and memory, it is not as effective specifically against depression as St.-John's-wort.[40]

I cannot emphasize enough the need for professional oversight in the area of supplement augmentation, especially if you have been nutritionally compromised by emotional, behavioral, or environmental factors. Restoring your optimum balance will prove well worth the time and energy.

Eating healthy and nutritional supplementation are excellent ways to give your body the resources it needs to combat your depression. These two strategies are so important, yet they are not the only strategies you can use to give your body a fighting chance to overcome your depression.

Physical Motion

Fat is a bad word. *Diet* is a bad word. *Exercise* is a bad word. That's why this section is entitled "Physical Motion." The reality is that most people don't exercise, but everybody moves.

Ben came to us tired, burned out, and overweight. His depressive state was producing negative effects in his marriage, and his wife finally had enough. She insisted that if Ben didn't want a divorce, he had to come in and work on their "issues." When he first arrived at the Center, the coercion was obvious on his face. He was there because he was forced to be, and he didn't hold out much hope for a successful conclusion.

Ben expected to be told how bad he was as a husband, how much of a failure his life was. Instead, he learned his wife really loved him and how deeply concerned she was about his depression. Instead of hostility, Ben received empathy and concern, from his wife and from his counselor. This support gave him the courage he needed to make some changes in his marriage and in his life.

He was counseled to move more. Ben's weight problems were due to his sedentary lifestyle. He sat at home. He sat at work. He sat in the car. He sat and watched television, with a remote. He sat and read the paper. If he needed something at home, he asked his wife or kids to get it. If he needed something at work, he snagged a subordinate. The more he sat, the larger, and the more unhappy and unhealthy, he became.

When their counselor first broached the subject of exercise, his wife had laughed and said Ben considered *exercise* a four-letter word. She said he considered a workout to be a trip down to the mailbox and back. While he didn't especially appreciate her laughter, he had to admit she was right. He just didn't like to exercise. Every time he tried to start something in the past, he failed. What was the point?

"Then, don't exercise," the counselor suggested. "Just move more." Moving more meant little things like not using the remote and actually getting up out of the chair to change the television channel. It meant parking a little farther away from his building at work. It meant using the stairs instead of the elevator. It meant doing his own errands instead of expecting everyone around him to do them. Moving more meant getting up after an extended period of time at his desk and walking around the plant. Moving more really wasn't that difficult. It got to where Ben really didn't even think about it. It wasn't long before he was playing with the kids in the yard before dinner.

No matter what you call it, physical motion or exercise is vital to a healthy life. It is also effective in relieving depression. The *British Journal of Sports Medicine* reported that walking thirty minutes each day alleviated symptoms of depression more quickly than many pharmaceutical antidepressants.[41] A Duke University study found that those who exercised were four times more likely to remain depression-free six months after the start of treatment than those who took medication.[42]

Like Ben, you may have difficulty imagining exercise as part of your life. You may have visions of gigantic weightlifters or slender long-distance runners and conclude you were never meant to be an athlete. What we are talking about here is not athletic competition. Rather, it is starting from wherever you are and gradually adding more motion. There is the saying, "Slow and steady wins the race." This is especially true for those who are just beginning to incorporate more physical activity into their day. Keep in mind the following principles:

- Start slow.
- Pick your motion.
- Maintain consistency.
- Use your journal.
- Find a friend.
- Be prepared for aches.

Start Slow

Oftentimes, a decision to start exercising is made in desperation and disgust. Desperation says, "Start now and start hard." Disgust says, "You deserve to feel bad." These twin voices come from frustration, and they doom our exercise attempts to fail. Why? Because, physically unprepared to begin at such a fast pace, our bodies and our spirits break down. We hurt. We ache. We quit.

By starting slow, we give our bodies a chance to catch up to our mental decision to begin exercising. Your brain says yes, but it's your body—muscles, joints, and tendons—that actually do the work. Starting slow allows your body and mind to develop cohesion and work together.

Pick Your Motion

When we are overcome by the twin voices of desperation and despair, we often choose the most inappropriate form of exercise to start with. Maybe it's taking up a sport from high school, only that was ten or twenty years ago. Maybe it's running instead of walking. Or singles tennis instead of doubles. Or one-on-one basketball instead of bowling. There is nothing wrong with running or singles tennis or basketball, but the timing isn't right. These are sports that require a certain level of fitness to be successful, or even safe. They are certainly something to aspire to, but if you haven't moved much for several years, you need to start out slow.

For many people, their first choice for increased physical motion is walking. Not speed walking or power walking, but simply getting out into the world and having a look around. Others will begin with low-impact aerobics or swimming. Others may modify a favorite activity, such as golf, and choose to walk part of the way instead of riding in the cart.

As you look for ways you can improve your health and your recovery from depression, pick out activities that you can enjoy. And for those of you who mutter that nothing involving exercise can be enjoyable, look for ways to find partial enjoyment. Do whatever it takes to get you moving.

Maintain Consistency

Physical motion needs to become a life choice. It's not about the next few weeks or the next few months or the next few years. It's about establishing a routine, a ritual, if you will, of being good to yourself through movement. In order to experience the maximum benefits, keep at it.

Consistency is not measured simply as an everyday event. Rather, you want to establish a new pattern. Start out by incorporating some sort of special movement, or exercise, every other day. If something such as an illness or injury prevents you from exercising for a while, don't listen to desperation and disgust. Cut yourself some slack, and start again when you are able—but be honest about when that is.

Use Your Journal

As you are integrating movement into your life, write down your thoughts and feelings in your journal. Allow yourself to explore how you are feeling before, during, and after you exercise. Note anything remarkable you discover. Oftentimes, physical movement can free up the mind to explore new avenues. It's as if while you are physically moving, you're giving the mind permission to wander. Because you want this physical movement to assist in your recovery from depression, let your mind wander, but keep the boundaries of your thoughts well within the borders of positive, uplifting ones. Reinforce those thoughts by writing them in your journal.

Find a Friend

If you find it a challenge to motivate yourself to exercise, ask someone to join you. It should be someone you feel comfortable with and who is at the same level, or slightly ahead, of you physically. If you don't feel like going out one day, perhaps you will find the motivation because of the other person. Personal interaction, as well as physical movement, is of tremendous value. You may soon find that you are going farther and doing more than you ever imagined because you are concentrating more on the other person than on the exercise.

If you need to choose a time of day that is inconvenient for other people, consider making a "friend" of a favorite radio station or an iPod. There are a wide variety of portable players specially made for use during exercise. Using a radio or an MP3 player can help you establish consistency by providing a "known" element to your exercise. You may not know what the weather is going to do, but you know you'll be listening to something you really enjoy.

Be Prepared for Aches

While it is important to start out slow, you don't want to stay so slow that you're not accomplishing anything physically. Ideally, you want to be able to work into an exercise routine that will produce a light sweat. Sweat is one of the main ways the body detoxifies itself.

As you push yourself, however, you will be working muscles, joints, and tendons that haven't been stretched in a while. As a result, you should experience minor aches and pains. These are normal and natural and are a sign you are working unused areas. Most aches should subside after a few days. It is possible to acknowledge the aches and continue to exercise.

As the muscles heat up and the body produces its natural opiates, the endorphins, the aches will subside during exercise.

While aches are to be tolerated, be aware of any pain. Pain is the body's signal that something is wrong. If you experience recurring pain doing one type of exercise, do something different. If walking or running is painful to your knees or hips, try swimming instead. The water will cushion your joints, and the heat will keep your muscles loose. Be aware of what your body is telling you—acknowledge aches but listen to pain.

If it has been awhile since you've engaged in any physical activity, consider going to your primary-care physician and obtaining a physical examination. For most of you, this won't be necessary if you're contemplating a walk around the block, but if you would like to incorporate anything more strenuous that you haven't done in years, go to your doctor. Ask his or her guidance in the type, duration, and frequency of an exercise plan.

Proper Hydration

It is only appropriate that after talking about physical movement we should talk about drinking enough water. The overwhelming majority of Americans don't. But how much is enough? A good rule of thumb is this: Half your body weight is the number of ounces of water you should be drinking every day. For example, a man weighing 176 pounds should be drinking 88 ounces, or 11 cups, of water each day. A 140-pound woman should be drinking 70 ounces, or just under 9 cups, of water each day.

This is *water* consumption, not *liquid* consumption. Many of the common liquids consumed today contain either caffeine or alcohol, both of which, as stated before, have a diuretic effect. They actually cause you to become dehydrated. Nor should you consume sugared drinks or even fruit juice. These can contribute to hypoglycemia by delivering large amounts of sugar into the bloodstream, triggering an insulin response. What you need to drink is water.

A Good Night's Rest

This may be difficult for you because a good night's rest is not something you *do;* it's something you experience. Depression interferes with the healthy production and operation of serotonin and melatonin, neurotransmitters used for the body's sleep-wake cycle. As you work toward recovery, you will want to assist your body in any way you can to achieve this restful sleep.

Try intentionally preparing for rest. This means allowing your body and your mind time to transition into sleep. Far too many of us carry on a stress-filled day right up to the time we climb into bed and then expect sleep to automatically arrive! This winding-down period could consist of listening to relaxing music, reading for enjoyment, listening to soothing natural sounds on an MP3 player or CD, or quiet meditation.

Give yourself enough time to get adequate rest. Eight hours, granted, is an average, but be aware of when your body might require more sleep. Anytime the body is under stress, physical or emotional, it will require more rest to rebuild and replenish. Five to six hours a night is probably not going to provide what you need. Resting adequately may require you to make choices about activities so you can establish a healthy routine of getting to bed on time.

Establish a set time to go to bed each night, whether weekdays or weekends. Studies show that it is far better for your sleep cycle to go to bed and get up each day at approximately the same time. You are helping your body to establish a biorhythm. If you swing from ten o'clock one night to two o'clock the next, your body is under stress having to adjust to wide swings of time. Do yourself a favor and find a time that works well for each day of the week, and then stick with it.

Cut out caffeine in the late afternoon and evening hours. Caffeine, as a stimulant, can interfere with your body's ability to know when it is actually tired. Instead of drinking coffee or caffeinated soda at dinner, drink some of your water or an herbal tea.

Reduce the activity, noise, and light levels as you go into the evening hours. Televisions blaring, lights blazing, and people running around frantically at ten o'clock at night is not conducive to rest. Start turning off lights, turning down volumes, and putting away activities as the evening progresses.

Another way you can help your body relax and ease into sleep is by not eating late in the evening. Evening snacking leaves food in your stomach that must be digested, and your entire body cannot fully rest if your digestive system stays up late to process your ten o'clock snack. One exception can be a small cup of hot tea, the kind that promotes a calming emotional effect. Or you may try warm milk.

Complementary Alternative Medicine (CAM)

In addition to therapy and, in some cases, prescription medication, there is another, more unconventional route to the treatment of anxiety, which is the number-one contributor to depression. These may include, but are not limited to

- Biofeedback therapies that are scientifically based
- Mindfulness-based therapy, which encourages a focus on the present-moment experience to alleviate anxious thoughts associated with the past or present or future
- Aromatherapy, particularly lavender oil
- Herbal remedies, which include a wide range of options, such as passion flower, kava, and lemon balm. Holy basil and schisandra are also effective, both of which are included in an herbal supplement I helped develop with Redd Remedies: InJoy, promoting healthy levels of neurotransmitters, supporting healthy mood regulation, and helping the brain and body cope with stress.

Though the effectiveness of the CAM approach is grossly understudied in comparison to prescription medications, the studies that *have* been done point to impressive results, with patients reporting a marked decrease in anxiety from treatment to treatment.

Moving Forward

Let's go over the five ways you can intentionally replenish your body:

- eating healthy
- nutritional supplements
- physical movement
- proper hydration
- a good night's sleep

To move forward in your recovery from depression, you will need to incorporate each of these into your daily routine. This won't be accomplished overnight and will require a commitment on your part to replenish your body. In order to integrate these lifestyle choices, give yourself sixty days. That's only two months' time.

Use Your Journal to Review Chapter 8

In your journal, map out the changes you are going to make week by week. Some you can start simultaneously. For example, if you are going to increase your physical activity level, you will want to be sure you are also drinking enough water. Set realistic, consistent goals for each week.

Tailor week two to build on week one. For example, you may decide you need to see your doctor before proceeding on an exercise program. You'll want to put calling your doctor for a visit into week one so you can begin to increase your physical motion in week two. If you need assistance deciding what supplements to take, seek that help in the first several weeks. You'll be ready in subsequent weeks to incorporate the supplements into your daily routine. If you've decided to improve your eating habits, you may want to "de-junk" your kitchen cupboards in week one so you'll be ready to eat healthier in week two.

As you look at increasing your water intake and your exercise level, write down your goals. Track your progress. Don't forget to be your own best encourager by writing down and reinforcing the positive steps you are taking to improve your health and recover from depression.

If you are hearing a small voice telling you it's too much work and too much hassle, don't listen. It is not that much work to choose an apple over a candy bar. It isn't too much of a hassle to keep a liter of water at your desk and drink during the day. It isn't too much work to get up and walk around and take a break at work. It isn't too much of a hassle to take a good multivitamin and mineral supplement each day with breakfast. It isn't too much work to tone down the level of your day each night. These are positive choices. You and your health are well worth it.

9

Renewing Your Spiritual Connections

God loves you—even when you're depressed.

Sunday morning. Great. Time to go to church and I'm fresh out of excuses. I used "not feeling well" last week and "out of town" three weeks ago. If I don't show up today, it'll be two Sundays in a row and someone will probably call or want to come over. But if I don't want to go to church on Sunday, I certainly don't want to talk about why to someone from the visitation committee during the week. So I'll just go—a little late and leave as soon as it's done. I won't show up on any list that way.

Okay, so I'm going, but I'm not dressing up. They should be happy I'm there at all.

Happy. Yeah, they'll be happy. We'll sing about joy, and they'll smile and laugh. If I keep a frown on my face and pretend like I'm rummaging through my purse, I can probably get out of there without anyone coming up to me after services. Happy people don't know what to do with a frown.

It's not that I'm mad at them. It's not their fault I feel this way. It's just so hard to sit or stand in the pew and sing about joy when I don't have any myself. I can't remember the last time I felt joy. I thought when I became a Christian, I was supposed to just become joyful, like God was going to wave a magic wand over me, causing all doubt and fear and loneliness and unhappiness to go away.

Well, if he did, it didn't work. I'm still unhappy, and I don't think I've ever felt so alone.

What's the deal? Where is God in all of this?

Finding the Connection

If you have ever had thoughts such as those expressed in the opening of this chapter, it may be comforting to know that God did not create us to live a life filled with sadness, fear, and depression. So as you have those thoughts of injustice—of *wrongness*—when you are feeling so depressed, you're right. You feel angry and frustrated and irritable for a good reason. You *weren't* meant to live this way—it *is* wrong. God's intention and desire for you is something completely different. The question is, how do you get from where you are to where he wants you to be?

Much of the book up to this point has been to help you understand why you are depressed. There are reasons, though they are not always apparent. Before you can get from where you are to where you want to be, you need to have a clear understanding of where you are and how you got there. This understanding is the basis from which to see a path to the future.

Understanding the reasons for your depression empowers you to direct your steps toward change. We have outlined the emotional, environmental, relational, and physiological reasons contributing to your depression. It is time for you to also understand any spiritual reasons. It may seem that the only spiritual connection to depression would be in helping you recover. However, depression can have deeply spiritual components, and it is imperative for you to discover what those are in your own life.

Spiritual Betrayal

If you have faith in God, depression can be similar to a betrayal by him. After all, you have trusted him to care for you, yet you are still depressed. You may have heard from your childhood that, as a Christian, you were to experience and exhibit joy, peace, patience—all the fruit of the Spirit spoken of in Galatians 5:22–23. This sense of betrayal may haunt your sleepless nights and invade your despairing thoughts. Feeling forgotten by God, you may even be angry at him.

This anger at God can contribute to your depression by provoking feelings of guilt. You don't think you *should* be angry at God, or you don't think you have *the right* to be angry at God, so you feel guilty when you are. You get angry when you pray and he doesn't fix it. The more you pray, the more you are convinced that he could fix it, but he won't. You don't understand why he won't. You doubt his love. But you've also memorized John 3:16, which begins, "For God so loved the world…" so you've been told he does love you. Looking at all of this, you conclude he's got a lousy way of showing his love, at least to you.

Or you may think, *Perhaps I don't deserve his love. Maybe he doesn't change my situation because I don't deserve joy and peace in my life. Possibly the things I've done are so bad that he wants to love me but can't because of who I am. And if God can't love me, then I'm not really worthy to be loved by anyone. And if my life is to be empty of love, hope is impossible.* If you look at it this way, depression is completely understandable. Or is it?

Have you picked up the stream of thought in this line of reasoning? It takes snippets of truth—God loves you, and Christians are to live lives of joy—and twists those around into something meant to injure you, not give you comfort. This line of reasoning is not from God; it is from the Deceiver. Rage is a deceiver. False guilt is a deceiver. Abject despair is a deceiver. Depression is a deceiver. That is why when you are in the midst of depression, you must replace your own negative self-talk with God-talk, which is based upon truth. This God-talk will support your positive self-talk by agreeing with affirming statements, such as these:

- I deserve love.
- I deserve joy.
- I am strong enough to learn and grow each day.
- I can experience contentment in my life.

- I am able to respond to my circumstances, instead of react.
- I can look forward to tomorrow.

To these, God adds his own response:

I deserve love: "For God so loved the world that he gave his one and only Son, that whoever believes in him shall not perish but have eternal life" (John 3:16).

I deserve joy: "Gladness and joy will overtake them, and sorrow and sighing will flee away" (Isaiah 51:11).

I am strong enough to learn and grow each day: "It is God who arms me with strength and makes my way perfect" (2 Samuel 22:33).

I can experience contentment in my life: "I have learned the secret of being content in any and every situation" (Philippians 4:12).

I am able to respond to my circumstances, instead of react: "Do not conform any longer to the pattern of this world, but be transformed by the renewing of your mind. Then you will be able to test and approve what God's will is—his good, pleasing and perfect will" (Romans 12:2).

I can look forward to tomorrow: "Because of the LORD's great love we are not consumed, for his compassions never fail. They are new every morning; great is your faithfulness" (Lamentations 3:22–23).

How do you fill your life and your mind with God-talk? The Bible is full of life-affirming messages. It is, at its heart, a love story. It is a story of a loving God, who created you to love you and to be loved by you. Like every great love story, there is a separation, which must be overcome by terrible sacrifice. Through God's sacrifice of his Son, Jesus, you are able to confidently say, "I *can* live happily ever after."

As good as these affirmations are, however, they must be supported by action. Positive self-talk and an acknowledgment of God-talk must be done even if you don't *feel* like it. Affirmations are action based not emotion driven. You must be able to understand and act out your knowledge of the role of love and joy in your life, even if at any given moment you do not feel joyful or lovable. How you feel about a truth does not alter its validity. God is the final judge of truth, not your response to that truth.

So, from a basis of God's truth, you can act upon these affirmations, despite your mood.

In the midst of your depression, listen to God instead of your despair. Fill your mind with promises and hope from his Word. At most Christian bookstores, you can find a book of God's promises, compiled around themes like love, peace, joy, hope, and forgiveness. This is an excellent way to keep the uplifting messages of God close to your heart.

You may want to obtain a copy of *The Soul Care Bible,* edited by Dr. Timothy Clinton. This valuable Bible is presented with editorial insights for those overcoming significant traumatic life events.

Be aware that not all religious-talk is God-talk. There are certain religious groups that stress manipulation, coercion, false guilt, and self-righteousness. What these groups produce is a toxic belief system that can lead to despair and depression as you try to live up to their ideal of "holiness." In this way, these groups exercise control over their followers and keep them cowering within their sphere of influence.

Freedom is found in God's truth and in his Word. Always measure what you are told by any religious group with the truth in Scripture. And don't let others tell you what the Bible says; read it for yourself. Remember, God wrote it just for you. (Please see the Resource List for the reference to *Toxic Faith* by Dr. Stephen Arterburn.)

There are reasons for your depression, but God desiring you to be unhappy and miserable is not one of them. God is not your adversary in depression but your greatest and most powerful resource for recovery. He is totally on your side in this struggle. But you must allow him to take control of the battle. You must follow his lead and not your own.

Forgive

By completing the exercises of self-evaluation in this book, you have achieved understanding about the reasons for your depression. You have discovered that there are some reasons you are responsible for, and some are due to the harmful actions of others. It can be very tempting to take these new discoveries and dwell on blame. But blame stops growth and traps you from going further. Blame doesn't want to move forward; it wants to dwell on the anger and pain.

You may blame yourself for decisions and actions you've made that contributed to your state of depression. You may be so hard on yourself for past mistakes that your depression sometimes feels like relief, that you are finally getting what you "deserve." Self-blame produces guilt and shame, and these may seem like "fair" compensation for what you've done wrong in your life.

You may blame others for the way their decisions or actions have hurt you and contributed to your depression. You blame others for simply not doing enough to help you or for being too wrapped up in their own problems to know you were hurting.

Circumstances, instead of people, can also be a focus of your blame. You feel the "odds" are against you or the "breaks" don't fall your way. You think, *The cards are stacked against me* or *Life just isn't on my side.* These are all rationales used to blame impersonal situations for personal problems.

On the road to recovery, blame is a dead end masquerading as a shortcut. Forgiveness, on the other hand, can appear to be a much longer, more difficult road to take. Forgiveness feels like a loss of personal control. But when you blame another person or circumstances, you turn power over to that person or circumstance. Forgiveness returns power to you because it puts you in charge. Forgiveness allows you to respond and not merely react. Blame is reactive, but forgiveness is responsive.

It can appear that forgiving people who have hurt you leaves you open to more pain. Forgiving is an action of control. By forgiving that person, you acknowledge her hurtful action and put her on notice that you are now in control of the relationship. With that control, it is up to you to decide the parameters you feel safe operating within. You can forgive that person of something in the past without granting her permission to hurt you in the future.

Forgiving others has another helpful benefit: as you learn to forgive others, it becomes easier to forgive yourself. But how do you know if you've actually achieved forgiveness? You can *think* you have forgiven someone, only to realize you still feel the pain of his offense when you are with him. You haven't enjoyed the freedom of true forgiveness if the anger, hurt, and resentment are still there. Seek to accomplish the following five goals as you work toward forgiveness:

1. I will not get even or do harm.
2. I have personal peace.
3. I will not engage in self-destructive behaviors because of this person or event.
4. I am able to put what has happened to me into the context of my present life.
5. I am able to accept myself and others.

Learn

As you remove the blame and guilt from your depression, it should make it easier for you to be open to learning what God has to teach you from it. God is the ultimate recycler—nothing goes to waste. He is able to use every experience, even your depression, to help you to grow. Chuck Swindoll, in his book *Hope Again,* puts it this way: "This variety of trials is like different temperature settings on God's furnace. The settings are adjusted to burn off our dross, to temper us or soften us according to what meets our highest need. It is in God's refining fire that the authenticity of our faith is revealed. And the purpose of these fiery ordeals is that we may come forth as purified gold, a shining likeness of the Lord Jesus Christ Himself."[43] Even amidst the fiery trial of depression, God is able to bless you and help you to grow. You must decide to meet him in this challenge for your life and learn more about him. Through difficult struggles, you learn about your true nature. You learn who makes up your true network of support. As you are comforted and supported, you learn about the steadfast love of the Lord.

Trust

Recovery from depression is not put on hold until you have everything figured out. Recovery is not a destination but a road that is walked. Some of the reasons for your depression will be evident, and some you may never completely understand. It is not necessary for you to wait until all the reasons are evident. Deeply buried answers take time to come to the surface, and God reveals truth on his own timetable. If you have to wait, you are not alone.

Hebrews 11 is a wonderful chapter outlining the trust of those from the Old Testament who never did see the fulfillment of all they hoped for. Yet they trusted in God and in his promises, even when they could not see. In the first verse of this chapter, there is this statement: "Now faith is being sure of what we hope for and certain of what we do not see." And again in verse 13: "All these people were still living by faith when they died. They did not receive the things promised; they only saw them and welcomed them from a distance."

There will be times on your journey when recovery looks distant. During these times, you must have faith that God is with you and trust his presence in your life. You must trust, even in the face of your own feelings. During these times, rely on Proverbs 3:5–6, which says, "Trust in the LORD with all your heart and lean not on your own understanding; in all your ways acknowledge him, and he will make your paths straight." Trust in the Lord, even when he seems far off, and he will help guide you out of your depression.

Obey

There will be times when you do not want to forgive or learn or trust. Depression is often a numbing response to one or more traumatic events. It can appear to be protecting you from feeling the full impact of the pain. As such, you may be reluctant to live life without it. A life fully lived is one where the full range of emotions is felt. After the gray of depression, the real world can seem bright and loud; it can hurt like coming out of a dark building into the sunlight. You may not want to come out.

At that point, you must allow obedience to supersede your desire. God wants you to come out into the light. Ephesians 5:8 urges us to "live as children of light." In order to do this, you need to forgive and forsake blame for your depression; you may need to learn some difficult truths about yourself or someone you love; you may need to trust God to comfort you when you've run out of hope.

Hope

In the midst of depression, hope may be the hardest trait to practice. Yet, hope is what prompted you to pick up this book. Hope urges you to turn this page. Hope whispers the surety of a better tomorrow. It is as fragile as a dream and as strong as a promise. Hope is the bedrock of your recovery from depression.

At the Center, we have a theme verse we use for ourselves and for our clients. It comes out of the Old Testament book of Jeremiah and speaks directly of hope. It says, "'For I know the plans I have for you,' declares the LORD, 'plans to prosper you and not to harm you, plans to give you hope and a future'" (29:11). Many of those who come into treatment for depression say they have run out of hope. They speak of trying many different avenues to find relief from their depression. Frustration is in their voices, but hope is in their eyes. If they didn't have some trace of hope, they would not be at the Center.

What they desperately need is someone to respond to and support that hope. They reach out to us one more time because over the years we have become known as "a place of hope." Romans 5:5 says, "And hope does not disappoint us, because God has poured out his love into our heats by the Holy Spirit, whom he has given us." Hang on to hope, and it will not disappoint you. That is a promise from God.

Hoping in a better tomorrow when crushed down by the despair of today can seem an impossible task. Yet, what else is there? All of these actions—to forgive, to learn, to trust, to obey, to hope—will require faith. Not the misguided belief in luck finally turning your way, but a solid assurance that God is in control and he loves you, even though you're depressed.

The Folly of Faith

Many of these spiritual concepts, such as hope and faith, are not understood through conventional, secular wisdom. Hope in the unseen. The Christian values of suffering, forgiving those who hurt you, and surrendering your will are inexplicable from the context of humanity. This is because these concepts were not formed in the crucible of humanity but on the altar of divinity. These are God's concepts, not ours. It is by his grace and love that he shares these concepts with us. Listen to God in Isaiah 55:6–9, 12:

> Seek the LORD while he may be found;
>> call on him while he is near.
> Let the wicked forsake his way
>> and the evil man his thoughts.
> Let him turn to the LORD, and he will have mercy on him,
>> and to our God, for he will freely pardon.
>
> "For my thoughts are not your thoughts,
>> neither are your ways my ways,"
>> declares the LORD.
> "As the heavens are higher than the earth,
>> so are my ways higher than your ways
>> and my thoughts than your thoughts...."
> You will go out in joy
>> and be led forth in peace."

Joy and peace are found in recovery from depression. They are not a daydream but a solid promise from a loving God. They are promised as you surrender yourself, and your depression, to him.

Moving Forward

It's time to explore your faith in your journal. Write down specific things you have been taught about God. Even if you were not a part of a religious organization, you probably picked up thoughts and impressions about God from the culture around you.

What were those thoughts and impressions? And where or whom did you get them from?

Do you still believe what you were taught or observed growing up? If so, why? If not, why not?

Do you consider yourself a person of faith today?

What truths about God do you hold on to at this very moment?

When you think about forgiving those who hurt you, what is your first impression? If you had a choice between forgiving someone else and forgiving yourself, which is easier for you? Why?

As you think about your depression, what do you think God is teaching you about yourself? about him? Are those things in alignment with what you know of the Bible? Do they reflect God's love, mercy, and forgiveness? If they do not, are you open to the possibility that they are not from God?

If it comes down to trusting God or trusting yourself, which would you choose? Are you able to tell the difference?

What things in the past have you entrusted to God? How did those things turn out? Are they more or less likely to encourage you to trust him again?

If you don't feel like you can trust God, what else or whom else do you put your trust in? What is the track record for those other things? If you feel like you can trust God, are you willing to turn over your recovery to him?

What do you hope for? What sort of future would you like to see for yourself?

What is your heart's desire? Do you believe that God will give it to you?

Psalm 37:4–5 says, "Delight yourself in the LORD and he will give you the desires of your heart. Commit your way to the LORD; trust in him and he will do this." Are you ready to commit your ways, including the reasons for your depression, to the Lord?

This road to recovery is more like a marathon than a sprint. It will take time because faith development takes time. James 1:2–4 says, "Consider it pure joy, my brothers, whenever you face trials of many kinds, because you know that the testing of your faith develops perseverance. Perseverance must finish its work so that you may be mature and complete, not lacking anything." God will do his part, and you must do yours by being patient as you work toward recovery.

Remember that evening and morning do not come all at once. There is a transition time from one stage to the next. As you consider your depression, realize that while a significant event may have happened suddenly, your state of depression probably evolved over time. Just as the sunlight of joy dimmed gradually, it will take time for the increasingly bright rays of hope, joy, and peace to permeate the gloom. Keep working. Keep trying. Morning will come.

Lord, give me wisdom. Open my eyes to learn. Thank you for your faithfulness and future victory. I will be patient. I claim your promise to lack nothing. I claim your hope.

Use Your Journal to Review Chapter 9

- Write down what you can remember learning about God while you were growing up. Be sure to indicate a source for each statement whenever possible.
- Write down what you believe God intends for your life.

10

Integrating the Whole Person

When you change your direction, you change your destiny.

The morning was overcast and gray, with a persistent drizzle that neither let up nor let loose. From the thickness of the cloud cover, Irene was sure it would be like this all day long. Undeterred, she grabbed a hooded coat from the closet before heading out the front door. *It's unrealistic,* she thought, *to expect sunny weather for every morning walk. I'm going to enjoy it anyway.*

A year ago, the weather would have sent Irene into a downward spiral, just further proof that the universe was out to keep her depressed. Her life had seemed as gray, as heavy laden as the clouds. Movement, motion, and motivation had been as hard to come by as a bright, sunny day in November. But that was last year. Over the past twelve months, Irene had been intentionally moving toward recovery from her depression. Her morning walks quickly became an integral part of that recovery.

She'd started walking to get some—any—exercise. It was also a way to get out of the house, which had recently become an empty nest with her last adult-age child moving out of state for a job. At first, it was all she could do to just get out the door a couple of mornings per week. She'd walked the way she did everything else back then, by rote, remotely.

It wasn't long, however, until she was able to get out more often, and she began to go farther. One of her kids got her a portable CD player, and

Irene found she actually enjoyed listening to music as she walked. Sometimes she would get lost in the music and the lyrics, and sometimes the music became a background for her own thoughts. She'd started to see a counselor, and her morning walks were the times she gave herself permission to really think about some difficult personal issues. On the weekends, her husband often joined her, and they spent the time going over the past week and planning for the week ahead.

This morning, Irene stopped briefly to admire the way the raindrops were gathering at the base of a scalloped petal on a neighbor's plant. It was simply beautiful, and she smiled at the thought that such a mundane thing could produce joy. Not that she disdained the joy but rather was astonished at its power and acknowledged how much she needed joy. Irene was coming back to life after a long, dark absence.

On her way home, she went over her plans for the day, recommitting herself to each as she recited them in her mind. Even the items that could be considered tedious, like grocery shopping, she decided beforehand were important and necessary. Lately, she'd started looking at grocery shopping as a grand hunt. After subsisting on mostly processed foods and far too much coffee, Irene realized she needed to change how she fed herself, and her husband for that matter.

When meal planning and cooking had become too overwhelming for her in the midst of her depression, her husband had taken over, with less than stellar results. Now she was glad she'd taken it back again. Shopping became a game almost, as she looked for good, wholesome foods. She'd even discovered new areas of her local grocery store and actually knew the name of the produce manager, who made it a point to stop and chat every time she came in. Often her husband would come into the kitchen at dinnertime, wondering what new thing she'd discovered, and they'd work together preparing the meal.

After the kids left, Irene felt as if her life unraveled. Now, thread by thread, it was weaving itself back together. With a sense of relief, she realized that hope, joy, and peace hadn't left her—they were still possible, they could still find her, even in unexpected places, even on rainy, dreary days.

As she walked up the driveway, Irene remembered a piece of paper in her purse. It had the phone number of a woman she'd met at church last Sunday. The woman wore the same look Irene had seen in the mirror too many times. *I'm going to call her today,* she decided. Irene finally felt enough joy to share.

Claiming a Purpose-Full Life

Congratulations on coming to this part of the book. You may have wondered if you would ever finish, or you may feel anxious now that you are nearing the conclusion. But the conclusion is not the end. On the contrary, this book is helping to put you in a direction that will change your destiny—away from your depression and toward hope, joy, and peace.

While this book sets you in the right direction, it is up to you to take action and move, one step at a time. There's a saying, "If it's going to be, it's up to me." That is how you must look at your recovery. You have the power to move from where you are to where you want to be. Now you will need to develop a purpose, plan, and mission for your life.

Purpose is what gives you the motivation to continue recovery, even when you don't feel like it. Purpose gives you the drive to keep going, no matter the challenge. Your own unique calling is your purpose. You may be uncertain what your purpose is, or you may simply need to recommit to it.

Like Irene, you may need to redefine your purpose. When Irene's children grew up and left home, she felt adrift. Up to that point, she had been living to provide for her children. Her identity and self-worth were locked into that task. When they left, so did her feelings of worth and motivation. As Irene worked with her counselor, she came to understand why she sought the safety of identifying solely with her children and what she needed to do to expand her view of the world and of herself. Rather than see her children's adulthood as a negative, she learned to see it as a positive, natural progression, and one that left valuable time for herself and for her neglected relationship with her husband.

If you have no idea what your purpose is, you are not alone. The famous psychologist William Marston once asked three thousand people the question "What do you have to live for?" Ninety-four percent of those who responded said they had no definite purpose. A lack of purpose causes a lack of passion. Passion is what energizes your spirit, and purpose gives you personal meaning.

Take out your journal, and spend the next fifteen minutes writing about your purpose in life. To help discover what it is, or what you would like to make it, answer the following question: "How do I want to be remembered?" I remember vividly doing this exercise at a critical time in my life. After thought and soul searching, I discovered my purpose is this: "To instill hope, encourage others, save lives and futures." This purpose frames my life—the decisions I make, the choices I take, the way I view those around me and myself.

Now it's your turn. You may not completely define your purpose in the next fifteen minutes, but you can get a good start. Place a marker in this page, put down the book, and answer the question "How do I want to be remembered?"

Integrating the Whole Person

Now that you are on your way to understanding your purpose, it's time for you to develop a plan to achieve that purpose. As I stated above, mine is "To instill hope, encourage others, save lives and futures." That would have been hard to accomplish if I refused to put myself in a position to be involved in the lives of other people. The results could have been disappointing if I had not prepared to meet the challenges of my purpose. Saying your purpose is progress, but planning for it is the next step.

You will develop a unique, personal purpose for life. But I encourage you to plan for a common purpose, which is to recover from your depression. After reading this book, you hold the whole-person keys to doing just that. But that purpose must evolve into action. It's time to look back over your journal and begin to put down concrete steps you are going to take to integrate what you've learned into your life.

Emotional Wellness

Go back and look at what you wrote, during the first chapter, on your emotional self. Through that section, you discovered some negative self-talk and destructive messages weighing down your ability to rise above depression. Your emotional-wellness plan is to intentionally replace those negative thought patterns with positive motivations. Basically, you are training your brain to think a different way. Because the more you think and dwell upon your depression, the worse it is.

Go back to the story that opened this chapter. Irene, before she went on her walk, needed to rechannel her thoughts from the negative to the positive. Do you see where? She reminded herself that it didn't need to be sunny to enjoy her walk. Irene could have looked outside, seen the weather, and decided to skip the whole thing. But she didn't fight with the weather; she accommodated her thinking to incorporate it. She changed the type of coat she wore and looked for the beauty in her surroundings. In this way Irene controlled the weather, instead of the other way around.

As you are working toward reorienting your self-talk from a negative range to a positive one, you need to consciously keep overwriting the negative messages that come so quickly to your mind. When negative messages arise, acknowledge them for what they are and root out their origins. Then intentionally replace them with positive messages that reinforce your purpose. Yes, it is going to be a drizzly day, but you will go about your purpose anyway.

Negative self-talk will keep you from even attempting something positive. I can't tell you how many times I have heard from people who were going to cancel an appointment with me because their negative self-talk told them it wouldn't really do any good, that nothing was going to make their situation better. Yet they overwrote that message with their strong desire to recover and move forward, even if they didn't understand how it was going to happen. They didn't want to come in, but they did, and afterward they were glad.

Negative self-talk always wins if it keeps you from trying. Counter it with the truth, and keep moving forward! If you need reinforcements in this battle, seek out a therapist or counselor to help.

Environmental Balance

Be aware that *what* you are doing affects *how* you are thinking. A rushed, frantic lifestyle contributes to fatigue and burnout, and it inflates the volume of negative self-talk. That is why it is so important to have environmental balance in your recovery. Look back over your journal entries for chapters 3 and 4. Set goals for realigning your activities. If you are doing too many things, it's time to provide yourself with the rest and recharging that you need to recover. If you have too much time on your hands, it is time to integrate meaningful, uplifting activities into your life. Each of these changes will require action on your part. Don't try to take on too many things at once. The goal is to keep moving forward.

Relational Healing

So much of the negative self-talk that fills our minds comes from dysfunctional relationships of the past. The activities we take on are a way to compensate for those negative messages. That is why it is imperative that you deal with any damaged or damaging relationships as you work toward recovery from your depression. In order to defuse the power of these dysfunctional relationships, purpose to forgive and move on. If a faulty relationship can be modified within the new boundaries you decide for yourself, then a continuation of that relationship is possible.

However, if a faulty relationship cannot be modified because the person refuses to honor your new boundaries, forgive and move on. Over time, that person may change and accept your new boundaries. If not, you have done all you can to heal while protecting yourself. Depending upon the relationship, look for other people in your life who could fill that void, and to whom you could give the treasure of your own relationship.

If it isn't possible to continue contact with a parent or sibling due to their behavior, look for an older person to act as a mentor or for someone your own age with whom you can develop a deeper friendship.

Physical Health

The body is an amazing creation with a remarkable ability to repair and heal. Give it what it needs to function, and the body responds in extraordinary ways. This does not happen overnight. Damage and deficiencies brought about over time must be healed over time. In physical recovery from depression, you must be patient. You must also be determined.

Perhaps you have turned to food as a way to self-medicate your depression. This causes an addictive response to the wrong types of foods or patterns of eating. Moving to proper nutrition and healthful eating will require a daily affirmation of your goals for recovery and physical vitality. You will need to remind yourself why it is good for you to avoid certain foods and choose others. You may need to alter your activities during the day to allow yourself time to properly feed your body. If you are suffering from a food allergy or environmental sensitivity, you need to obtain professional help to address this issue in your life. Remember, your body has been a partner to your depression, and you must make it an ally in your recovery.

Spiritual Renewal

We are creatures of flesh and blood, but we are also spirit. Faith and belief in yourself and in your recovery are important for success. Depression is not merely an emotional upheaval or a physical condition; it is a spiritual assault on the truth of God's love, the promise of his care and concern, and his desire for you to experience an abundant life.

Belief and faith are twin anchors when the mundane threatens to drag you down. When you don't feel like loving yourself, God still does. When you don't feel you are worthy of recovery, Christ declares your worth through his death. When you don't have the strength to continue, God offers his through his Spirit. God remains the source of truth.

If depression has caused you to move away or hide from God, change direction and seek the Lord. Go right to the source, his Word and his Spirit. Incorporate spiritual commitment and discovery into your healing from depression.

Tech Detox

No thorough examination of whole-person living would be complete without attention to one of today's biggest threats to balanced living—our tech-intensive lifestyle. Almost every waking moment, we are either in front of or within arm's length of one of possibly numerous tech devices. From smartphones to laptops to iPads, our attention is chronically drawn somewhere else, perpetuating a way of living that is difficult and dangerous to sustain.

Physically, our frequency of use of all these tech devices takes a toll. Your neck, back, and wrists suffer from working on a computer all day. Your physical activity is naturally limited when the focus of most waking hours is in sedentary positions in which the predominant motion involves your fingers. And your overall health is proven to be at risk from exposure to cell phones which may be carcinogenic.

Mentally, our tech-intensive lifestyles promote increased levels of multitasking. After all, the more devices you have to connect with, and at increasing speeds and with improved functions, the more you can accomplish. Of course, that is the irony of it all. The same devices intended to simplify our lives only serve to make room for us to squeeze more to-dos onto the list.

Relationally, all the connecting we're doing online is only further *dis*connecting us from the people who matter most—our family and friends. Physically, we may be present—at meals, in the car, or just hanging out at home—but most of the time, you or someone with you is on a tech device. Chances are the goal is to strengthen an online relationship via Facebook, text, or e-mail. Meanwhile, we're actively ignoring the opportunity to strengthen our relationships with loved ones right in front of our faces.

If any of this rings true for you, it's time to take action. You need not disconnect completely, but merely be mindful of your actions, experimental with changing them, and flexible with how you envision your tech time in the future.

Use Your Journal to Review Chapter 10

- Write down what you believe to be your purpose in life.
- Answer the question "How do I want to be remembered?"
- Keep going. Don't give up.

11

The Personal Recovery Plan

You are not your thoughts.

Every night, Melissa marveled that another day had passed without her anxiety throwing her into depression. It's not that the anxious thoughts weren't there. In fact, they came and went all day long. The difference was she had finally learned to recognize them as such—just thoughts about her life, not life itself.

Just one year ago, any number of undesirable circumstances could have sent Melissa into a tailspin—a bad date, a disagreement with a friend, an unexpected expense, criticism of her work, a to-do list out of control. But now, when the obsessive thoughts of "I'm not good enough…smart enough…together enough" came up—in all their various incarnations—Melissa had learned to *observe* these thoughts instead of *absorb*ing them.

"I am not my thoughts" had become a common mantra. And when that wasn't enough, distracting her mind did the trick, with a walk, a run, a nap, a journal entry, yoga, meditation, or a visit with a close friend.

It's as though Melissa's mind and body had learned to live on an autopilot she could finally trust, observing and diffusing negative thoughts before they manifested into negative emotions. This was something she had never experienced in all her forty years, only now coming to realize that "down" days here and there every couple of weeks didn't reflect the normal ups and downs of life everyone experienced, but bouts with depression that she had learned to circumvent with the help of therapy, mindfulness, courage, and faith.

Claim Your Recovery

In your journal, write down on separate pages "Week 1" through "Week 12." Give yourself three months to integrate what you've learned through this book. Write down what your own personal plan looks like for the next twelve weeks under the five subheadings of Emotional Wellness, Environmental Balance, Relational Healing, Physical Health, and Spiritual Renewal. Under each of these categories, determine how to move forward in each for the next twelve weeks.

Realize that these goals are not set in stone and may need to be revised over the next three months, as long as you continue to move forward and make progress. Inaction is not an option. Inaction will not enhance recovery. Most likely, you have been depressed for at least three months. Isn't it worth giving recovery at least as much time as you've given your depression? If you are confused about what this twelve-week plan might look like, here is a sample for you to consider.

Your Personal Recovery Plan

Week One

Emotional Wellness—Go through the Resource List at the back of this book and choose a book that connects with your individual situation. Over the next month, commit to reading and integrating this book into your life.

Environmental Balance—Choose one negative activity in your life and decide why it is negative for you. As you engage in the activity this week, consider whether you want to eliminate it altogether. Is there a way to modify that activity to make it less negative?

Relational Healing—This first week, work on forgiving yourself for your depression. Consider the relationships in your past or present that have contributed to your depression. Realize the futility of blame, and try to treat yourself with care and concern.

Physical Health—If you are experiencing significant health problems, call this week for an appointment with your family doctor, and ask about the type, duration, and frequency of recommended physical activity. What you learn will help you plan for the remainder of the three months, and beyond.

Spiritual Renewal—Get a Bible, if you don't already have one, and pick a theme verse for your recovery. Try looking in the concordance in the back of the Bible for verses with certain keywords, such as *hope, joy,* or *peace.* Make sure your choice reflects the way God feels about you, not the way you feel about yourself. If you have trouble finding a theme verse, you might try praying Mark 9:23–24, which paraphrased says, "Everything is possible for those who believe. Help me overcome my unbelief." Memorize your verse this week, and use it during the day to keep focused on recovery.

Tech Detox—Keep a detailed record of your connected activities. Where are you connecting, for how long, and what are you doing there? Include e-mail, texting, Facebook, Twitter, browsing, searching, and any other plugged-in aspect of your life. Calculate your time at the end of the week for each category, then add them all up for one total comprehensive number of how much of your time is devoted to connected activities in one week's time.

Week Two

Emotional Wellness—Continue reading through the book you have chosen. If you are able, consider speaking to a pastoral counselor or a professional therapist. Be sure to highlight passages in the book that strike close to home for discussion or personal reflection this week.

Environmental Balance—Continue to think about the negative activity you chose during the first week. Is this activity negative because of your perceptions? Try participating in this activity from a positive point of view. This week, observe whether this change improves the situation.

Relational Healing—Think of a relationship you really value. It may be a past or current relationship. Why is this relationship so special to you? Attempt to contact the other person and express your gratitude for the relationship. It doesn't need to be excessive, just a note of thanks or a phone call. Allow the other person to respond, without expectation. The goal is not their response but your acknowledgment of the value of the relationship. Let that goal stand on its own.

Physical Health—Incorporate physical activity into your daily routine. Start by choosing a time of day that works for you on a regular basis. Now decide what the activity will be. It could be walking, biking, or swimming. It may be something you remember from your past that gave you pleasure. Start slow and allow yourself time to build.

Spiritual Renewal—Choose a scripture dealing with hope. This will be your verse for the week. Memorize it and say it, along with your verse from week one. You don't need to memorize it word for word, however. If it is easier to remember and has more meaning, put the verse in your own words. Read through Psalms this week during times of quiet reflection. Consider memorizing Psalm 62:5: "Find rest, O my soul, in God alone; my hope comes from him."

Tech Detox—Look back at last week's log of your connected activity. Note *where* and *when* you are spending your time, *what* you're doing there, and for *how long*. Next note how you feel about it. And how do those feelings affect how and what you may want to change? Do you want to cut down on your texting? Do you want to lessen the frequency of your Facebook posts? Do you want to set aside fewer times a day to check your e-mail? Take your time with this goal-setting task, as it will help shape the next ten weeks of your tech detox. Write down your goals, and review them regularly in the weeks to come.

Week Three

Emotional Wellness—Continue working through your chosen book this week. In addition, keep a small notepad nearby. Write down every time negative self-talk rears its ugly head. Write down the message, and counter it with a positive one. Develop a consistent response each time the same negative message recycles itself.

Environmental Balance—Look at your activities, and evaluate the number and frequency of positive ones. Choose one thing you'd really like to start doing, and make whatever plans are necessary to begin next week. If it's taking a class of some kind, find out this week what is involved and enroll.

Relational Healing—Choose another positive relationship in your life this week to focus on. Express your appreciation for the relationship this week.

Physical Health—Look through your kitchen, and evaluate the foods you are eating. Cut back on processed foods, and eat more whole foods. Pick out a different whole food each day this week. Begin taking a good multivitamin, and increase your water intake.

Spiritual Renewal—If you are not attending a religious service during the week, make plans to attend. Look in the newspaper, or make calls to those in the area that interest you. If you do attend services, recommit to going this week. Use time this week to prepare yourself spiritually for the worship experience.

Tech Detox—Refer to the list of goals you made last week. Pick one to focus on in week three. Remember, this may include cutting down on texting, limiting your Facebook posts, and checking e-mail less frequently. Be specific, though, in your goal. For instance, "This week I will only send three texts a day. If I need to communicate more with someone, I will call him instead." Or "This week I will only post to Facebook once a day and only check my newsfeed twice a day." Or "This week I will set aside thirty minutes in the morning and thirty minutes in the evening to check and respond to e-mail." Beyond this limiting of tech time, equally important is replacing it with something else. Every day incorporate an alternate activity into your life, such as taking a walk, meeting friends for lunch, playing ball with the dog, meditating, or reading a book.

Week Four

Emotional Wellness—You should be nearing the end of your chosen book. Discuss the ideas or concepts with a trusted friend, a pastoral counselor, or a professional therapist. Continue to work on overwriting negative messages with positive affirmations.

Environmental Balance—Start your new activity this week, if you have not done so already. Be open to the new experience and any new people with whom you come into contact.

Relational Healing—Seek out a positive relationship in your life that can be expanded. Perhaps this is someone in a work or social situation that values you as a person but with whom you haven't had the opportunity to spend a lot of time. Make plans this week to get together with that person. Find out what that person enjoys doing, and join in.

Physical Health—Continue substituting whole foods for processed foods in your diet. Drink more water as you drink less caffeine and/or alcohol. Be sure to maintain your daily multivitamin and any supplements. Go through your house and eliminate unneeded chemicals. Allow fresh air into your house or workspace each day.

Spiritual Renewal—This week, purpose to pray every day upon waking and each night before sleeping. Keep a journal of your prayers. If you are unfamiliar with prayer, consider using the ACTS method: adoration to God; confession of sins; thanksgiving for his blessings; and supplication, or asking for what you need.

Tech Detox—Record your thoughts and feelings about last week's tech detox. How successful were you at sticking to your goals? If you slipped, what was the trigger? On the days when you were successful, how did it feel being less tech intensive? Were you anxious? Did it feel like you had more time on your hands? Does this inspire you to continue limiting your connectivity? Why or why not?

Week Five

Emotional Wellness—Congratulations! You are beginning your second month of intentional whole-person recovery from depression. This week, concentrate on acknowledging the positive effects in your life and on being thankful.

Environmental Balance—Continue with your new positive activity. Recommit yourself to that activity.

Relational Healing—Now that you have spent the past month strengthening your relationship with yourself and being grateful for the positive relationships in your life, it is time to consider the negative relationships. If there are negative relationships you would like to salvage, take time this week to think about them. If you have done things to damage these relationships, take responsibility for them and make contact with the other people.

Physical Health—Keep moving, keep drinking water, keep eating healthy, keep taking your vitamins. As you are able, increase your level of each. Remember, you don't want to plateau but move forward. Continue to work with your health-care professional on any lingering physical condition that may be hindering your ability to become more physically active.

Spiritual Renewal—Look in the Resource List in the back of this book. Choose a book that interests you. Go to your local Christian bookstore, and find a book that touches your heart. You might start with a book by Max Lucado, whose beautiful prose puts God's love into immediate, personal context. Allow the book to speak to you of God's forgiveness, love, and mercy. Keep repeating your theme verses. Add verses from your reading. Allow God to speak to you.

Tech Detox—Look back at your goals from week two. Choose another to focus on this week. Remember to be specific. For instance, "This week I will only send three texts a day. If I need to communicate more with someone, I will call her instead." Beyond this limiting of tech time, remember to replace it with something else. Every day incorporate an alternate activity—an outing, a hobby, time spent with friends or family.

Week Six

Emotional Wellness—Identify one area that you continue to struggle with. Look at this issue from all angles this week, but don't allow thinking about this hurdle to deter you from forward motion. You are like a high jumper sizing up the next jump—not to become discouraged, but to prepare yourself to leap high and clear the top. Use those who are helping you whenever possible.

Environmental Balance—If your life has been full of chaotic activity, adding a new activity these past few weeks may be a bit of a strain. Look over your list of activities, and choose a negative one to drop in favor of the new positive one. This negative choice could also be inactivity. As you begin to regain your emotional strength, new activities will cease to be stressful and will become energizing.

Relational Healing—Make it a point this week to acknowledge your part in the damaged relationships you identified last week. If possible, express your responsibility directly to the person. If not, do so in a letter. If the person is still alive, mail the letter. If the person is not, keep the letter to review it as you decisively gain closure on that relationship.

Physical Health—Don't let up on your commitments. Choose this week to tackle one thing you've been finding hard to do. Focus on it this week, and try to discover why it is so difficult. Continue to look over your home and your workspace to find ways to let in more natural light and fresh air. Breathe new life into your home and your workspace. Consider adding a piece of new furniture or a fresh coat of paint. Ask someone you trust to look over these spaces with you, to help think of ways to renew them and make them alive. Consider purchasing full-spectrum light bulbs for your bathroom or kitchen.

Spiritual Renewal—Continue working through the book you purchased last week. Consider switching radio stations to a Christian one, or purchase Christian CDs or download a style of music you enjoy, and listen to it in the car, at home, and at work, if possible. Keep praying and reading your Bible.

Tech Detox—Record your thoughts and feelings about last week's tech detox. How successful were you at sticking to your goals? If you slipped, what was the trigger? On the days when you were successful, how did it feel being less tech intensive? How did this week's detox focus differ from the previous one? Was it easier or harder? How and why? Of the two tech detoxes you have now completed, which one feels like it was the toughest to endure, and what makes you think so?

Week Seven

Emotional Wellness—Take a run at overcoming the difficult hurdle that you identified last week. Realize you may not completely make it over the top. Don't be discouraged if you fail the first time. In competitions, contestants are often allowed two attempts. Shouldn't you get at least the same break in life?

Environmental Balance—Each day this week, write down something unusual or unexpected or previously unnoticed in your physical surroundings that brings you joy or pleasure.

Relational Healing—Prepare yourself this week for a response from the person with whom you have taken responsibility for a damaged relationship. If that person responds in a healthy, appropriate way, then reconciliation can begin. If that person responds in a way that is harmful or destructive, reiterate your personal boundaries. Do not allow this to become a battle of wills. You are in the process of cleansing yourself from the damage of the relationship. If the other person is not willing to do likewise, the relationship cannot go forward. Prepare to put it behind you so you can continue moving forward.

Physical Health—Continue the things you know are good for you: activity, proper eating, nutrition, and hydration. At this point, you should be experiencing the benefits of the fifth physical goal: restful sleep. If this is not the case, talk to your health-care professional. It's also a good time to reevaluate any supplements or medications you are taking.

Spiritual Renewal—Consider making an appointment to talk with a spiritual advisor, if you have not done so already. Be open about your depression. Pray together and seek God's wisdom and direction as you continue on your recovery.

Tech Detox—Look back at your goals from week two. Choose another to focus on this week. Remember to be specific. For instance, "This week I will only post to Facebook once a day and only check my newsfeed twice a day." Beyond this limiting of tech time, equally important is replacing it with something else—like going for a run, spending time in the garden, or baking a cake!

Week Eight

Emotional Wellness—It's time to take a personal inventory of your strengths and weaknesses. Determine if a particular weakness is holding back your recovery from depression. It could be a tendency to procrastinate or a desire for perfection. Share this weakness with someone you trust, and begin to formulate a plan to change.

Environmental Balance—Purpose this week to spend some time alone in quiet surroundings. If possible, spend several hours going to a museum or public garden. Specifically choose a quiet, restful place, and allow your thoughts to wander. Enjoy the solitude.

Relational Healing—Think about the outcome of last week's encounter. If it was positive, be thankful and spend some time this week journaling what this reconciliation can mean in your life. If it did not go as you had hoped, acknowledge the reality of the relationship, and write about the impact of closure and what it will mean in your life. Determine if there are any circumstances under which you would continue this relationship as it presently stands.

Physical Health—Begin to implement any changes to your routine, as recommended by your health-care professional. If things are going well, keep going. This is a lifestyle change you are working on, not a short-term fix.

Spiritual Renewal—Choose a theme verse for this week that reflects where you are spiritually. Finish the book you are reading.

Tech Detox—Record your thoughts and feelings about last week's tech detox. How successful were you at sticking to the goal? If you slipped, what was the trigger? On the days when you were successful, how did it feel being less tech intensive? How did this week's detox focus differ from the previous ones? Was it easier or harder? How and why? Of the three tech detoxes you have now completed, which one feels like it was the toughest to endure, and what makes you think so?

Week Nine

Emotional Wellness—Continue with your plan for addressing a personal weakness. Be aware of each time it interferes with your commitment to continue. Document these bumps in the road, and write down a simple strategy you will use next time to work around it and move forward.

Environmental Balance—Last week you purposefully spent time in quiet reflection. This week, you will want to purposefully take time to play. Go to a sporting event or comedy club. Your goal this week is to laugh! A lot!

Relational Healing—Spend extra time this week with a positive person. This will be helpful if the encounter of two weeks ago did not go as well as you'd hoped. Realize there are uplifting, strengthening relationships out there for you. Purpose to become a better friend to the positive people in your life, recognizing their value and importance to you.

Physical Health—Go to the Resource List in the back of this book. Pick out a book that emphasizes good health or nutritional eating. Begin reading this book and using its recipes and suggestions.

Spiritual Renewal—Invite someone to lunch after services this week. Pick up the check. Be open to God's leading as to whom that person should be. Confirm your faith with that person and be open, if it seems appropriate, about what you are going through.

Tech Detox—Spend a week limiting your time and activities on *all three* of the online activities you previously addressed. These need not be the same exact goals you already set for each, but may be amended based on what you learned from the previous experiences and how you would like your future activity to look.

Week Ten

Emotional Wellness—Continue countering your personal weakness with intentional action. Often, these personal weaknesses have taken years to develop. Persistence, patience, and forgiveness will be vital. If you're working with a counselor, discuss your struggle to overcome in this area of your life.

Environmental Balance—Look over your current activities, and examine whether you have any that put you in contact with those less fortunate than you. Are any of these "giving" activities? Consider volunteering at a service club, a local elementary school, or the public library. Being aware of the needs of others can help put your own situation into proper perspective.

Relational Healing—Take time this week to consider how your relationship with yourself is going. How are you feeling about you? Is there an area of your life where you simply need to forgive yourself for something you've done and then move on? If there are any "would-haves," "should-haves," "could-haves" holding you back, it's time to let them go. Acknowledge them, learn from them, and move forward.

Physical Health—Continue to work through your book, and experiment with new ways to introduce healthier choices into your life. Try out a new grocery store this week, or go to a farmers' market. Taste something new.

Spiritual Renewal—Last week you focused on you and someone else. This week, focus on you and God. Be aware this week of his presence in your life. Call on his name throughout the day. Visualize him walking with you this week. Invite him into your life and your thoughts. Maintain a constant sense of prayerful contact.

Tech Detox—Record your thoughts and feelings about last week's tech detox. How successful were you at sticking to your goals? If you slipped, what was the trigger? On the days when you were successful, how did it feel being less tech intensive? How much more challenging was it to limit multiple sources of connectivity as opposed to just one? Are these all sources you may like to continue limiting in the future? If not, why not? Are there other connectivity areas in which you feel you could use some limitations?

Week Eleven

Emotional Wellness—This will be a week of reflection in many areas. Spend time this week reflecting on the progress you've made. Allow yourself to enjoy your accomplishments. Don't try to minimize them or react to them with false modesty. You want to celebrate!

Environmental Balance—Focus this week on the positive aspects of each activity, even those that are difficult or tiring. Look for the silver lining in every cloud. During or at the end of each activity, acknowledge the positives and be thankful.

Relational Healing—Be thankful for your family this week. Spend time thinking about each family member and listing all of the positive qualities you see in them. Include those people who operate as family members to you, especially close friends who may have taken the place of a father, sister, or brother.

Physical Health—Pamper your body this week. Take a nice, hot bath or shower. Get a professional massage or facial. Every time you get out of bed this week, be grateful for your improving health.

Spiritual Renewal—Continue reading through your book, as well as God's Book. Read the stories of Ezra and Nehemiah in Scripture, about the rebuilding of the temple. Consider your recovery from depression to be a rebuilding task. Look for analogies between the two. Allow God to speak to you through his Word.

Tech Detox—Try a week without limits to your connectivity. Give yourself the freedom to check, post, and play to your heart's desire. As in week one, keep a detailed record of your connected activities. Where are you connecting, for how long, and what are you doing there? Include e-mail, texting, Facebook, Twitter, browsing, searching, and any other plugged-in aspect of your life. Calculate your time at the end of the week for each category, then add them all up for one total comprehensive number. How does this number compare to the one from week one? Is it less? More? And how do you feel about that?

Week Twelve

Emotional Wellness—Map out where you'd like to be in three months. If this level of writing and planning has been helpful, continue it as long as you need to. Keep working with your counselor and moving forward toward emotional healing and recovery.

Environmental Balance—Look ahead to activities coming up, especially those centered around a specific time of year or holiday. Determine if there are any changes you want to implement now, before those activities actually arrive. Inform anyone necessary of your change in plans. Be prepared to explain how this will be beneficial for you, then stick with your decision.

Relational Healing—Go out and have your picture taken, but not alone. Choose one of your relationships, be it a spouse, child, friend, or extended family member. Use the occasion of the portrait to reemphasize how important that person is to you. It doesn't need to be a formal portrait to be special. Take a candid shot, if appropriate. Go to a favorite place, and ask for help capturing the moment. Be sure to give the other person a copy.

Physical Health—Recommit to taking good care of yourself. Remind yourself every day this week to be kind to your body. Be careful what you do to it and for it, as well as what you put into it. Remember to work in harmony with your body as you continue to recover from your depression.

Spiritual Renewal—Give your continued recovery over to God. Ask for his direction as you go into your next three months. Pray every day this week for strength to continue, motivation to overcome setbacks, and vision for the way ahead.

Tech Detox—Look back over your logs, thoughts, and feelings for the past eleven weeks. Based on what you have experienced and felt, what boundaries would you like to set with regard to your tech time in the future? Make a list of goals to incorporate into your daily life. As with this formal, guided tech detox, be sure to record your thoughts and feelings about the experience. It's important to check in with yourself to note where you are having success, what you can do better, and how you feel about it. It's all about trial and error; as with anything else, you can't know what works and what doesn't until you try it.

Realize that the preceding twelve-week plan is a guide only. You may move ahead more quickly in one area or need more time at a certain juncture. It is your recovery, and the goal is forward motion. It is not a race to see how fast you can get to the finish line. Allow yourself to be an individual. Just remember to keep *moving forward*.

Notes

1. World Health Organization, "Depression," Media Centre Fact Sheet no. 369, October 2012, www.who.int/mediacentre/fact sheets/fs369/en/index.html.
2. Centers for Disease Control, quoted in "Examining the Broad Reach of Depression," CBS News *Sunday Morning,* March 18, 2012, www.cbsnews.com/8301-3445_162-57399521/examining -the-broad-reach-of-depression/.
3. According to Ronald Cowan, MD, PhD, an instructor in psychiatry at the Harvard Medical School, nearly twice as many women (12 percent) suffer from depression in any given year as men (7 percent).
4. Lindsey Tanner, Associated Press, "Treatment for Depression on the Rise," *Seattle Post-Intelligencer,* January 8, 2002, www.seattle pi.com/national/article/Treatment-for-depression-on-the-rise-10 76817.php.
5. Sy Safransky, ed., *Sunbeams: A Book of Quotations* (Berkeley, CA: North Atlantic Books, 1993), 144.
6. Dr. Reinhold Niebuhr, quoted in "The Origin of Our Serenity Prayer," Alcoholics Anonymous History and Trivia, www.aa history.com/prayer.html.
7. Erica Westly, "Psychiatric Drugs Replacing Talk Therapy," *Scientific American,* December 2, 2008, www.scientificamerican. com/article.cfm?id=psychiatric-drugs-replacing-talk-therapy.
8. Peter R. Breggin, MD, *Toxic Psychiatry* (New York: St. Martin's, 1994).
9. Breggin, *Toxic Psychiatry,* 17.
10. Peter R. Breggin, MD, *Talking Back to Prozac* (New York: St. Martin's, 1995).
11. Breggin, *Talking Back to Prozac,* 230.

12. "Ketamine Improved Bipolar Depression Within Minutes, Study Suggests," ScienceDaily, May 30, 2012, www.sciencedaily.com /releases/2012/05/120530100247.htm.

13. "Causes of Depression," WebMD, www.webmd.com/depression /guide/causes-depression.

14. Daniel Amen, "12 Ways SPECT Scans Can Help You Pt 1" video, Amen Clinic, www.amenclinics.com/index.php/dr-amen /media/category/spect, and www.amenclinics.com/conditions-pro /anxiety-depression-pro.

15. Robert A. Anderson, MD, *Clinician's Guide to Holistic Medicine* (Columbus, OH: McGraw Hill, 2001), 243.

16. "Treatment-Resistant Depression," Mayo Clinic, www.mayo clinic.com/health/treatment-resistant-depression/DN00016.

17. L. Pauling, "Orthomolecular Psychiatry: Varying the Concentrations of Substances Normally Present in the Human Body May Control Mental Disease," *Science* 160 (April 19, 1968): 265–71, summarized at U.S. National Library of Medicine National Institutes of Health, www.ncbi.nlm.nih.gov/pubmed /5641253.

18. M. J. Park, S. W. Yoo, B. S. Choe, R. Dantzer, and G. G. Freund, "Acute Hypoglycemia Causes Depressive-Like Behavior in Mice," *Metabolism* 61, no. 2 (February 2012): 229–36, summarized at U.S. National Library of Medicine National Institutes of Health, www.ncbi.nlm.nih.gov/pubmed/21820138.

19. Gina Kolata, "Which Comes First: Depression or Heart Disease?" *The New York Times,* January 14, 1997, www.ny times.com/1997/01/14/science/which-comes-first-depression -or-heart-disease.htm.

20. James M. Greenblatt, MD, "The Breakthrough Depression Solution: Is Gluten Making You Depressed?" *Psychology Today,* May 2011, www.psychologytoday.com/blog/the-breakthrough -depression-solution/201105/is-gluten-making-you-depressed.

21. Michael Downey, "Block Food Cravings at Their Molecular Root," *Life Extension Magazine,* August 2012, www.lef.org

/magazine/mag2012/aug2012_Block-Food-Cravings-At-Their
-Molecular-Root_01.htm.

22. "Hypothyroidism and Depression," WebMD, www.webmd.com
/depression/hypothyroidism-and-depression.

23. "Don't Overlook Your Thyroid," *Life Extension Magazine*, August
2012, an article excerpted from *The Fatigue Solution* by Eva
Cwynar, MD, www.lef.org/magazine/mag2012/aug2012
_Dont-Overlook-Your-Thyroid_01.htm.

24. James M. Greenblatt, MD, "The Breakthrough Depression
Solution: Can a Simple Blood Test Solve Depression?" *Psychology
Today*, October 2011, www.psychologytoday.com/blog/the-break
through-depression-solution/201110/can-simple-blood-test-solve
-depression.

25. "Low Testosterone Levels Associated with Depression in Older
Men," ScienceDaily, March 4, 2008, www.sciencedaily.com
/releases/2008/03/080303190624.htm.

26. David Freeman, "Are Allergies Making You Depressed?" WebMD,
www.webmd.com/allergies/features/allergies-depression.

27. Carl C. Pfeiffer, PhD, MD, *Nutrition and Mental Illness: An
Orthomolecular Approach to Balancing Body Chemistry* (Rochester,
VT: Healing Arts, 1987).

28. William G. Crook, MD, *The Yeast Connection* (New York:
Vintage, 1986).

29. P. F. D'Arcy, "Adverse Reactions and Interactions with Herbal
Medicines, Part I: Adverse Reactions," *Adverse Drug Reactions
and Toxicological Reviews* 10, no. 4 (1992): 189–208.

30. Richard A. Passwater and Elmer M. Cranton, *Trace Elements,
Hair Analysis and Nutrition* (New Canaan, CT: Keats, 1983).

31. Syd Baumel, *Dealing with Depression Naturally* (Lincolnwood, IL:
Keats, 1998), 42.

32. "Drugs That Cause Depression," WebMD, www.webmd.com
/depression/guide/medicines-cause-depression.

33. Jesse Lynn Hanley, MD, and Nancy Deville, *Tired of Being Tired:
Rescue, Repair, Rejuvenate* (New York, G. P. Putnam's, 2001), 64.

34. "Investigating CAM Approaches to Generalized Anxiety Disorder," *Life Extension Magazine,* Summer 2012.

35. Emma Cale, "Folic Acid and SSRIs," September 1, 2011, Live Strong, www.livestrong.com/article/528294-folic-acid-ssris/.

36. M. Fava, J. S. Borus, J. E. Alpert, A. A. Nierenberg, J. F. Rosenbaum, and T. Bottiglieri, "Folate, Vitamin B12, and Homocysteine in Major Depressive Disorder," *American Journal of Psychiatry* 154, no. 3 (March 1997): 426–28, summarized at www.ncbi.nlm.nih.gov/pubmed/9054796.

37. James M. Greenblatt, MD, "The Breakthrough Depression Solution: Is Your Depression Linked to Low DHEA Levels?" *Psychology Today,* July 2011, www.psychologytoday.com/blog /the-breakthrough-depression-solution/201107/ is-your-depression-linked-low-dhea-levels.

38. Stacy Jordan, "How to Raise Your Serotonin Levels Through Diet and Amino Acid Supplementation," September 28, 2010, LiveStrong, www.livestrong.com/article/250012-how-to-raise-your -serotonin-levels-through-diet-amino-acid-supplementation/.

39. "St. John's wort (Hypericum perforatum L.)," Mayo Clinic, www .mayoclinic.com/health/st-johns-wort/NS_patient-stjohnswort.

40. M. Gideon Hoyle, "Ginkgo Biloba and St John's Wort," May 19, 2010, LiveStrong, www.livestrong.com/article/126533-ginkgo -biloba-st-johns/.

41. F. Dimeo, M. Bauer, I. Varahram, G. Proest, and U. Halter, "Benefits from Aerobic Exercise in Patients with Major Depression: A Pilot Study," *British Journal of Sports Medicine* 35 (April 2001): 114–17, http://bjsm.bmj.com/content/35/2/114.full.

42. Isabel Walker, "Fighting depression: aerobic exercise is proven to be more effective than antidepressants." Peak Performance, www .pponline.co.uk/encyc/fighting-depression-aerobic-exercise-is -proven-to-be-more-effective-than-antidepressants-214.

43. Charles R. Swindoll, *Hope Again: When Life Hurts and Dreams Fade* (Nashville: W Publishing, 1996), 19.

 Resource List

Battles Men Face: Strategies to Win the War Within by Gregory Jantz, PhD (Grand Rapids, MI: Revell, 2012). Exposes the temptations that can entrap good men and gives practical steps to overcome unhealthy patterns. Shows how to accept who you are (and who you're not), build on the positive, and, perhaps most difficult, ask for and accept help.

The Body God Designed by Gregory Jantz, PhD (Lake Mary, FL: Strang, 2007). Presents the idea that God himself made you and has a body intended just for you. Includes healthy models for each body shape; principles for effective, long-term weight loss; how to stop secret and mindless eating habits; differences between healthy and unhealthy fats and where to find each.

The Cognitive Behavioral Workbook for Depression: A Step-by-Step Program, second edition, by William J. Knaus, EdD, and Albert Ellis, PhD (Oakland, CA: New Harbinger Publications, 2012). Includes worksheets and exercises for evaluating depression and tips on preventing relapse.

The Depression Cure: The 6-Step Program to Beat Depression without Drugs, reprint edition, by Stephen S. Ilardi, PhD (Cambridge, MA: Da Capo Lifelong Books, 2010). Addresses depression from the perspective of our busy, twenty-first century lives. Suggests treatment that forgoes the use of prescription drugs.

Every Woman's Guide to Managing Your Anger by Gregory Jantz, PhD (Grand Rapids, MI: Revell, 2009). Explores ways to overcome anger and use it positively in life, including how to accept the truth of anger; examine where it comes from; be honest about how it's

used; be open to change; be willing to forgive even ourselves; and
be willing to feel something besides anger.

Get the Sugar Out, second revised edition, by Ann Louise Gittleman,
PhD, CNS (New York: Three Rivers Press, 2008). Sugar-cutting
tips with multiple uses that can be used time and time again until
they become habits and maybe even family traditions.

God Can Help You Heal by Gregory Jantz, PhD (Lincolnwood, IL: Publications International, 2006). Includes inspiring insights to help
with healing from physical addictions, broken relationships, and
past abuses.

Gotta Have It!: Freedom from Wanting Everything Right Here, Right Now
by Gregory Jantz, PhD (Colorado Springs, CO: David C. Cook,
2010). Uncovers the truth hiding behind secret desires.

Happy for the Rest of Your Life by Gregory Jantz, PhD (Lake Mary, FL:
Strang, 2009). Explores our misconceptions about what happiness
is and where to find it, dead ends on the road to happiness and how
to avoid them, and why God is really the author of "Don't Worry,
Be Happy."

Healing the Scars of Emotional Abuse by Gregory Jantz, PhD (Grand
Rapids, MI: Revell, 2009). This revised and expanded edition includes strategies for dealing with a verbal abuser, self-check quizzes,
keys to rebuilding relationships, stories from survivors of emotional
abuse, new information on spiritual abuse, and a biblical plan for
healing.

How to De-Stress Your Life by Gregory Jantz, PhD (Grand Rapids, MI:
Baker, 1998). Designed to pave the way to renewed physical, emotional, and spiritual health. Reveals eight secrets for finding all the
energy you'll ever need, ways to eliminate self-defeating attitudes,
and more.

*The Mindful Way Through Depression: Freeing Yourself from Chronic Un-
happiness* by Mark Williams, John Teasdale, Zindel Segal, and Jon

Kabat-Zinn (New York: The Guilford Press, 2007). Four experts on depression address the mental traps that can cause and perpetuate depression, including rumination and self-blame.

Overcoming Anxiety, Worry, and Fear: Practical Ways to Find Peace by Gregory Jantz, PhD (Grand Rapids, MI: Revell, 2011). Compassionate combination of common sense, biblical wisdom, and therapeutic advice. Helps readers identify the causes of anxiety, assess the severity of symptoms, and start down avenues for positive change.

Potatoes Not Prozac: Are You Sugar Sensitive, updated edition, by Kathleen DesMaisons, PhD (New York: Simon & Schuster, 2008). If your brain and body chemistry overreact to sugar and simple carbs, this seven-step process can help.

Self-Coaching: The Powerful Program to Beat Anxiety and Depression, second edition, by Joseph J. Luciani, PhD (New York: John Wiley & Sons, 2001). The emphasis here is on the negative thought patterns that contribute to anxiety and depression and how to develop a new, positive way of thinking to allow the reader to make healthy choices. The self-coaching refers to a self-talk technique to counter old, destructive ways of thinking.

Sugar Blues by William Duffy (New York: Warner Books, 1975). A classic bestseller that alerted the public to the addictive and toxic effects of an overabundance of sugar in the diet, leading to conditions ranging from heart disease to depression.

The Testosterone Syndrome: The Critical Factor of Energy, Health, and Sexuality—Reversing the Male Menopause by Eugene Shippen, MD, and William Fryer (New York: M. Evans, 2001).

Toxic Faith by Dr. Stephen Arterburn and Jack Felton (Nashville: Thomas Nelson, 1991).

Undoing Depression: What Therapy Doesn't Teach You and Medication Can't Give You, second edition, by Richard O'Connor, PhD (New

York: Little, Brown, 2010). The author looks at genetic, biochemical, and environmental factors but also delves into the role our own habits play in depression. It teaches how to use new skills to replace old patterns of negative thinking, behaving, and relating.

What the Bible Says About Healthy Living: 3 Principles that Will Change Your Diet and Improve Your Health by Rex Russell, MD (Ventura, CA: Regal, 2006). This book outlines three principles for healthy living: eat the foods God created for you, don't alter God's design, and don't let any food or drink become your god.

The What Would Jesus Eat Cookbook by Don Colbert, MD (Nashville: Thomas Nelson, 2011). This cookbook uses biblical principles of eating to promote weight loss, prevent disease, enjoy balanced meals, and gain health. It emphasizes whole foods that are low in salt, fat, and sugar, as well as high in nutritional value, and that taste good.

The Yeast Connection Handbook by William G. Crook, MD (Garden City Park, NY: Square One, 2007). An overgrowth in the body of a simple yeast, *Candida albicans,* is shown as the culprit in a variety of chronic, devastating health problems, including depression. Solutions to curb this overgrowth are included, as well as a detailed presentation of the science behind the theory.

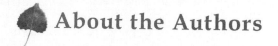 # About the Authors

Gregory L. Jantz, PhD, is a popular speaker, award-winning author of more than twenty-five books, licensed mental-health counselor, certified chemical-dependency professional, and certified eating-disorder specialist. He is the founder of the Center for Counseling and Health Resources, a leading health-care facility in Washington state (Aplaceofhope.com).

Dr. Jantz's "whole person" approach to recovery addresses the emotional, physical, intellectual, relational, and spiritual dimensions of human beings. His compassionate, solutions-oriented viewpoints on timely topics, plus a natural gift for storytelling, make him a sought-after guest on local and national radio and television. He has authored numerous books, available through his website at Drgregoryjantz.com.

Ann McMurray is a freelance writer living in Brier, Washington. She has coauthored numerous books with Dr. Jantz and participates in the work of hope at the Center.

For more information or if you would like to talk to someone, please call our toll-free number: 1-888-771-5166.
You can also contact us on our website, www.aplaceofhope.com, to sign up for our newsletter, or you can contact us by mail at
The Center for Counseling and Health Resources
PO Box 700
Edmonds, WA 98020

There is hope...
people can and do change

For 28 years, **The Center for Counseling and Health Resources** has been known for its individualized, confidential, whole-person philosophy.

- Rediscover freedom from depression and anxiety.
- Recover from anorexia, bulimia and binge eating.
- Rebuild after traumatic events.
- Reclaim your life from addictions.

Call 888-771-5166 to speak to an admissions specialist.

The Center
for Counseling and Health Resources Inc.